HOLLYWOOD'S ENDURING LEGEND SPEAKS OUT...

ON HIS TEMPER: I don't know what has given me this terrific reputation... If you ask someone about one of my so-called flare-ups, they'll usually say, "Oh, we heard it from..."

ON JOHN WAYNE: Wayne has very prescribed concepts as to what he should play, whereas I feel an actor should play anything.

ON BURT LANCASTER: He's fun. He's aggressive. Sparks fly. I like that. We always had fun. *Loud* fun.

ON HIS SON, MICHAEL: A pretty girl ran up to me on a plane with a lovely look in her eye. Then she asked me, "Hey, are you really Michael Douglas's father?" I'm delighted at Michael's success.

ON ACTING: I'm looking for new challenges in acting. Maybe it's being a child again, because acting is a childish profession.

AUTHOR MICHAEL MUNN is a leading show-biz journalist who contributes to numerous publications. Entering the film industry at age 16, he worked for Cinerama, Warner Bros., and Columbia before turning to full-time writing. He is the author of *The Stories Behind the Scenes of the Great Film Epics* and *Tony Curtis—The Kid From the Bronx*.

KIRK DOUGLAS

Michael Munn

ST. MARTIN'S PRESS/NEW YORK

Kirk Douglas was first published in Great Britain by Robson Books Ltd.

KIRK DOUGLAS

Copyright © 1985, 1989 by Michael Munn.

Cover photos by Gamma Liaison.

Library of Congress Catalog Card Number: 85-50208

ISBN: 0-312-91370-2

Printed in the United States of America

St. Martin's Press hardcover edition published 1985
First revised St. Martin's Press mass market edition/March 1989

10 9 8 7 6 5 4 3 2 1

CONTENTS

Introduction

It's not often that anybody throws a grand Hollywood party for Kirk Douglas. Indeed, it's not until quite recently that Douglas became an endearing enough personality to warrant such a party. But in 1983, when he turned sixty-seven, Kirk was honorary chairman and guest of honour at a tribute for him at which he was awarded the Albert Einstein Award from Israel's Institute of Technology. Among the famous guests were Robert Mitchum, Gregory Peck and Ernest Borgnine. The event proved to be a veritably star-studded edition of 'This Is Your Life' as Kirk's colourful and often controversial life and career were retold for the benefit of all, not least, I suspect, for Kirk himself.

Perhaps the highlight of the evening came when into the spotlight stepped Burt Lancaster, Kirk's long-time friend and colleague. So warm and deep is the affection which they have for each other that their public greeting was movingly a full kiss on the lips.

Turning to the audience Burt said, 'I've worked with him many times over the span of years, and I think I know him pretty well. Let me start by telling you something about him. To begin with, he is the most difficult and exasperating man that I know—except for myself.'

With that the audience laughed knowingly and applauded. Burt continued: 'He fights with his wife, he fights with his children, he fights with the maid, he fights with the cook. God knows, he has fought with me!'

Lancaster continued to detail many of the events in Kirk's life, after which Kirk rose and said, 'As I listened to my life story, I thought, "What a wonderful movie it would make." And there is only one person to play it—Burt Lancaster.'

Kirk was really speaking affectionately of his friend, and not of himself: Kirk really doesn't see his own life ever serving as the plot of a film or novel. He once told me:

> I've always said that my life is a B-script. I never want to make a movie out of it because it is too typical of what one thinks of as *the* American story. You know—Russian immigrants who can't read or write come to America. Their son is growing up and working his way through University, and going into the work that he's chosen. It's all sort of cornball. Although it has happened often, I don't want to imply that every American immigrant's son can just grow up and become a millionaire movie star.

Douglas, surprisingly, undersells himself. His life is certainly much more than B-movie material. It's true that his story is somewhat typical of the rags-to-riches variety. But there is a difference. Most movie stars who were taken out of the gutter at an early age and pushed into the limelight of Hollywood and covered from head to toe in tinsel, were generally dependent on some guardian angel, or Svengali, or just on some talent scout with a good nose for potential fame.

Kirk Douglas was dependent on nobody. Everything he achieved he did on his own. He fought his way to the top, displaying an aggressiveness and a drive that tended to split Hollywood into two camps—those who were pro-Douglas and those who were anti-Douglas. While he has won many friends he has also earned probably more enemies than any other American actor. He has admitted, 'I don't think I'd ever win any popularity contests in Hollywood. But I don't think I want to.'

There is only one thing that really interests Douglas, apart from his family. That is making good pictures—good *Kirk Douglas* pictures. And his track record speaks for itself. He has a good nose for box office. He also has a much ignored versatility as an actor, as will be seen. But perhaps more than anything, he has proved to be a good businessman. Over the years he has earned a fortune by producing, packaging and selling himself. It's probable that he would have succeeded in any career he may have chosen. If he had started out as a humble tailor, I'm sure he would have ended up owning a huge garment factory; if he'd been a miner, he would probably have bought the mine eventually. As it happens, Kirk Douglas chose to become an actor, and he ended up owning his own production company and even got to direct a couple of his own films.

That Kirk Douglas should achieve stardom should not, in retrospect, be surprising. His success is the fulfilment of childhood desires to be something more than just a street urchin. As Kirk himself observed, 'When you start at the very bottom, there is nowhere else to go but up.' Douglas also had something else going for him—something that comes from thousands of years of Jewish ancestry: the zeal to be his own master and the classical Jewish ability to succeed in business. These are attributes which eluded his father whose only function in Kirk's success story was to act as a catalyst driving Douglas, even as a boy, to become a champion.

M.M.

ONE / Issy

Kirk Douglas came into the world as Issur Danielovitch on 9 December 1916, in Amsterdam, a town in New York's Mohawk Valley where his Russian parents, Herschel and Bryna Danielovitch, came to live after they arrived in America in 1910. Issur, or Issy as he was known, escaped being born into the repression and persecution of Russia by just six years.

In their native Russia, Herschel and Bryna had lived among their fellow Jewish proletarians in an impoverished village south of Moscow. For all Jews it was a time of terror; they lived under the constant threat of violence. The government had openly encouraged anti-Semitism since 1881 when a Jewish student girl was involved in the assassination of Tzar Alexander II. Gentile mobs demonstrated their prejudices with no interference from the government, and the Jews became subject to laws which restricted them to certain occupations and forbade them to own land.

Jewish communities became targets of Jew-haters who organized themselves into bands of marauders, bringing death and destruction to villages and towns. These pogroms began with the dreadful Kishineff massacre of 1903 and became more frequent following the suppression of the Russian Revolution of 1905. These pogroms resulted in houses of Jews being burnt, Jewish women being raped, and the mutilated bodies of Jews left to litter the streets.

Over the centuries since they had left Palestine, the Jews had been persecuted and driven out of other lands. During the fourteenth century they were expelled from Britain and France, and Eastern Europe became the only area where they were allowed, for a time, to reside in relative safety. But now they were again being forced to leave. There was economic depression in Russia at the time of these pogroms, brought on by the Russo-Japanese War and the ensuing revolution, causing the tide of non-Jewish emigration from Russia to rise just as sharply as the Jewish exodus.

It was under these conditions of dire poverty and the never-ending threat of death that Herschel and Bryna lived. In 1910 they joined the fleeing throng of Jews, desperate to leave a country where starvation was now becoming a greater threat than the pogroms. Over a period of years, 30,000 of these Jews had managed to migrate at last to Palestine where the Zionist movement had been active since 1897. But the numbers were restricted by the Turks, and so a greater number of Jews crossed the sea to Argentina where they found they could live relatively peacefully. Great Britain also became, for a time, a new promised land, but there hostility towards Jews fleeing from Eastern Europe steadily grew until the government shut the immigration doors.

There was one place left to go—America. There immigration was virtually uncontrolled. Furthermore, it was a land which for years had inspired myths in the minds of the Jewish proletarians of Russia. Bryna would, in later years, admit to Issy that she had been brought up on stories of how the streets of America were littered with golden bricks.

Passage to America by steamship had become easy and cheap due to the tremendous competition among steam shipping lines. Herschel and Bryna were able to book their passage, and after a long, sea-sickened voyage, they arrived in the harbour of New York. The tremendous influx of immigrants was ushered into the federal buildings newly erected on Ellis Island, to be questioned and inspected by immigration officers.

The Danielovitches were hardly any different from the thousands of other illiterate Jewish peasants who were seeking entry into the United States. Herschel had no skill in any trade but was a physically powerful man who believed he could find some way to use his strength in earning a living. They soon discovered that there was no gold in the streets of New York. Instead, there were thousands upon thousands of other Jews, all as desperate as they. By 1914 more than 90 per cent of all Jewish emigrants from Eastern Europe had settled in the United States. New York was not only the first stop for the immigrants, but for most of them it was also the last stop. The State of New York became the home of most incoming East Europeans whether Jewish or gentile. Neither was there any gold in the town of Amsterdam where Herschel and Bryna settled. However, so grateful were the Jews just to be there that to them America was always their *goldene medire*—their golden land.

Amsterdam was basically a one-business town where two companies, Mohawk Mills and Sandford Mills, had the monopoly on the carpet trade. Herschel, totally illiterate and unskilled, was unable to secure work at either of the mills. However, he did manage to find work of a kind peddling fruit and fuel. It was a time-consuming, meagre-wage-earning job, traipsing through the streets for hours every day with an old horse and cart, peddling goods. Herschel hardly earned enough to feed and clothe his ever-growing family.

By the time Issy was born, six years after Herschel and Bryna first settled in America, he already had three sisters. Within the next few years three more sisters would be born. Issy soon came to hate being the only male of seven offspring, and even as a small boy the thought of escaping from a female dominated household was beginning to take root in his mind. He says:

> We laugh at it now, but it was terrible being the only male in a house full of women. I was dying to get out. In a sense, it lit a fire under me. It's said that an actor is the kind of actor he is because of his childhood and his life experiences, and that it's only possible to gauge his strength and his weaknesses in view of that background. I think this is certainly true in my own case.

Right from the beginning Issy sported that famous dimple of his. 'As a matter of fact,' he points out, 'my father and my mother had a dimple. My six sisters have the same. Actually, it's a weakness of the muscle. It's so perfectly formed, some people think I had it put there.'

In the State of New York, truant officers really had their work cut out for them. Children of school age were constantly failing to turn up to be educated, and as the East Europeans flooded in, so truancy increased. There was no great mystery. The truant officers discovered that it was not the children but the parents who were responsible for absenteeism in school. Fathers, unable to provide a decent income, were sending their children to work in factories or to shine shoes in the street in an effort to supplement their pitiful earnings.

So it was that Issy, hardly more than a small boy, was sent out by his father to earn an extra dollar or two. To the mills Issy would go, selling soft drinks and sweets to the workers, many of whom were hardly more than kids themselves. An average day's earnings usually allowed Issy to purchase some milk and a loaf of bread for the family to dine on that evening. On a good day, Issy earned enough to buy two quarts of milk and a couple of packets of breakfast cereal. Then the Danielovitch family would enjoy the luxury of cornflakes for dinner. So scarce was food that nobody in the family ever left scraps on their plate. Eating every mouthful was a habit which Issy would retain all his life, even when times were good.

One day Issy was fortunate enough to find a potato lying in the street. He picked it up, but this time he didn't take it home. He showed it to a friend of his who was just as hungry, just as poor. They lit a fire in the gutter, slowly baked the potato over it, and relished it. It's memories like this that prompt him to say, 'Unless you've been hungry-poor, you don't know what poor means.'

Issy didn't go without an education. Bryna always encouraged Issy to take full benefit of the American education system, and she had aspirations of him going to University. Herschel was more interested in sending his son out to work, and in the ensuing years Issy would take on more than forty different jobs before earning a living as an actor.

In the years to come Kirk Douglas would not be able to look back on his early life and recall any incidents with the glowing nostalgia with which many tend to enhance their recollections.

For him there never were 'the good old days'. The good days were yet to come.

He once said:

> People are often actors because it's a form of escape from the real world. And I had plenty to escape from, believe me. When I look back on my life I realize I had a pretty tough childhood. My parents were Russian immigrants who couldn't read or write when they came to America. It was I who taught my mother to write her name. My father peddled fruit in New York, and in his spare time had us children. Seven in all. Six girls and me. It was one helluva struggle, and there were times when we weren't sure where the next meal was coming from.

Although Kirk continues to remind the four sons he now has, about how hard he had it all, he manages to be slightly self-derisive. 'You can almost hear the violins in the background,' he says, 'in this tale of a lad from the bottom rungs of society climbing his way to the top of the ladder.'

When Kirk Douglas did escape from the life of Issur Danielovitch, he was never inspired to make a pilgrimage back to the street where he sold pop and candy to the mill workers. 'I never have that it-gets-you-right-here feeling when they play the school song,' says Douglas.

Much of the sadness in the life of the boy they called Issy was caused by his father Herschel, who never was given to displaying love or pride in his children. In fact, Issy grew to resent his father's indifference towards him. Issy was a rather puny little kid, while his father was a tough, rough character who was just about the best fighter in the neighbourhood. Never at any time was Herschel moved to put an arm around his son and express any warm feelings he may have had. That Herschel seemingly failed to feel any love and pride in his son's achievements simply served to drive a wedge between father and son, although in his early years Issy was far too intimidated by his father to display his resentment and disdain openly. Herschel simply made Issy feel that he could achieve nothing in life, and so secretly Issy grew ever more determined to be *somebody*.

15

Issy's mother, on the other hand, was like a loving hen who gathered her children about her and protected them with her wings as best she could. She also recognized in Issy the potential to reach beyond himself and achieve things that others would have found hard to believe him capable of. Bryna probably first recognized this when Issy, at the age of just five, took part in a presentation at school in which children from Kindergarten joined with the first grade kids, of which Issy was one, to entertain teachers and parents with various playlets and poems. Bryna knew Issy to be a shy, sensitive, easily intimidated boy, and yet he was given the assignment to stand alone and recite a poem solo. It was a harrowing experience for the small boy to get up in front of all those staring eyes and eager ears, but because of the environment in which he lived and which he hated so much, Issy had learned to use his imagination to escape to a fantasy world and make it believable for him alone.

He nervously began his poem. It told of the red robin of spring, and as he spoke the words, pictures formed in his mind and for a few moments he was carried away into a fantasy of birds and sunshine and countryside. He spoke now with confidence and assurance, and he believed everything he said. When he finished, the audience applauded enthusiastically. For the first time in his life, Issy felt that he had actually done something to touch people in a way that made them respond positively. It was then, he says, that 'an actor was born'.

With his mother's support, he nurtured his ability and desire to act, and when he went to Wilbur Lynch High School in Amsterdam, he came under the careful eye of his teacher, Louise Livingston, who was quick to note the boy's talents. In no time at all she had him reading theatrical literature, and encouraged him to enter speech competitions and to take part in debating teams. Bryna was delighted with his progress and readily gave words of encouragement. Herschel, however, seemed totally unimpressed. Then one evening, Issy, unable to keep his resentment pent up any longer, made a small but significant display of contempt.

The whole family was seated around a table. Herschel, who wasn't home much these days, was in a foul mood. He sat drinking tea Russian style from a glass, sucking the tea through a sugar cube which he gently but firmly clenched between his teeth.

Issy sat watching the moody patriarch. Herschel looked so mean, so powerful, while Issy felt so small and puny next to his father.

Something inside Issy suddenly snapped. He couldn't bear to suppress his resentment any longer. He felt as if he would burst unless he did something.

He scooped up a spoonful of tea, took aim, and flicked it right into Herschel's face.

The next thing Issy knew, big, rough hands were picking him up off his chair and effortlessly throwing him, like a rag doll, through the air. He sailed through an open door and landed shaken, winded—but safe—on a bed. He lay there for a few moments, scared to death, glad to be in one piece, but very proud at having stood up to his father at last.

'It was the moment,' he says, 'when I too became a man.'

TWO/
/Early Gambles

The boys and girls of Amsterdam were abuzz with excitement, but none more than Issy when the news broke that Sanford Mills was sponsoring a public speaking and acting competition. The most outstanding orator or actor would be the lucky recipient of a special medal.

With his mother and Louise Livingston giving him moral support, Issur Danielovitch was Amsterdam's most enthusiastic entrant. He chose not to recite from a play, but to do the self-same thing he had done in the first grade which initially inspired him to pursue dramatic activities: to recite a poem. This time it reflected his more mature years; he was thirteen. No robins and sunshine for this occasion. It was to be a poem called *Across The Border* which told of a mortally wounded soldier and the thoughts which haunt him as he hovers between life and death.

On the big day, Issy, now confident and self-assured, was word-perfect and, more importantly, he brought the poem to life. It was a performance which won him the medal, an award which probably meant more to him than all the other accolades he would gain as an international movie star, because this was the very first award.

At the time of the competition, Issy was working part-time as a store clerk for the Goldmeer Wholesale Company. He worked every evening and Saturday. When he won his medal for public speaking, his employer was so impressed with the boy's talent that Issy was asked to give a special performance for the benefit of the Goldmeer salesmen. It was a tough assignment for the youngster, but he carried it off with the cool aplomb of a professional, belying his shyness and insecurity at being on show for his superiors.

Issy continued to pursue his oratory and dramatics activities as well as excelling in academic studies. He had a fine mind, and his mother continued to encourage him to apply to enter University, but after he graduated from high school at the age of seventeen, his father completely abandoned the family: any thoughts of going to college now appeared to be dashed, as it fell upon Issy and his three older sisters to provide for the rest of the family.

Issy found a full-time job as a clerk at Lurie's Department Store, giving almost every dime he earned to his family, but managing to keep some back for himself—he was saving to pay his way through college. By the end of the year, though, all he had was a hundred and sixty three dollars: University now seemed out of the question.

Then, on sheer impulse, Issy decided to try something desperate. A gamble! The first real gamble of his career. He planned to come face to face with the Dean of St Lawrence University at Canton, New York, and somehow convince the Dean to give him a chance. It was a long shot. But he had everything to gain and nothing to lose.

He donned his best suit and began hitch-hiking his way to Canton. After riding in a variety of vehicles who offered to take him as far as they were going, Issy found himself making the last stage of the journey on top of a truck carrying manure. He arrived at the University smelling of fertilizer and in a rebellious mood because of his odour. He found his way to the Dean's office, and when he entered the Dean almost fell off his chair at the foul aroma.

Issy explained that he had hitch-hiked all the way from Amsterdam to see if he could enrol at the University. He explained also about the truck-load of manure.

The Dean explained that he could find no application form from young Danielovitch.

Young Danielovitch explained that he hadn't sent one. He'd not even phoned to make an appointment. All he had was his high school credentials. He was also broke, desperate and eager to further his education.

The Dean cast his eyes warily over Issy. Then he silently read over Issy's high school reports. Something about the young man impressed the Dean. It certainly wasn't the aroma, but the sheer determination which Issy had thus far demonstrated. The Dean looked up at Issy and announced that he was willing to give him a chance. Issy was overjoyed. He had hardly dared to hope that this hair-brained scheme of his would actually work. Not only was he to enter University, but the Dean also arranged for Issy to take a loan from the college.

The first thing Issy did was to go and find himself a job as a part-time gardener at thirty cents an hour. In a short time Issy was fired when it became apparent that although he had arrived in town smelling like a garden, he certainly didn't possess green fingers. However, he quickly found himself another job, as a janitor. Unable to afford to rent a room in the college dormitory, Issy spent the nights at his janitor's quarters. He learned quickly to live on his wits and cunning. And friendship. Sitting with his pals in the college restaurant, he'd eat the bits and pieces they'd pass to him.

Issy worked hard throughout virtually every waking hour. If he wasn't studying, he was working as a janitor. But he occasionally found time to relax, and even attended a few college dances without having to buy a ticket. He simply checked the college sick list to see who was too ill to go to the dance, and if no one suitable was listed—if none had dance tickets—then he'd talk any known campus hypochondriacs into visiting the infirmary by insisting that they didn't look well enough to go to the dance. Then he'd do them a favour by taking their ticket rather than see it wasted.

The shy, intimidated child was quickly evolving into a forceful young man. He even tried his hand at wrestling, and ended up as the undefeated champion of St Lawrence University and title-holder of the Intercollege Wrestling Championship. Desperate for extra money, Issy decided to put his wrestling skills to a more financially profitable use. He landed a job during the summer holidays at a carnival wrestling ring. He'd pose as a member of the audience, and when the villain of the bout began to break all the rules and beat his opponent to a pulp, Issy would jump into the ring, rip off his jacket and shirt, and challenge the bad guy to a match. Issy usually won too. Reflecting on those days, Kirk Douglas wryly comments, 'I guess I really learned to act in the wrestling ring!'

Actually, it wasn't just in the wrestling ring that Issy displayed his talent as an actor. He performed in many University stage productions, including *Death Takes A Holiday* in which he was billed not as Issur Danielovitch, but Isadore Demsky. Issur Danielovitch, he reasoned even then, was not a name to stick in the minds of audiences. His enthusiasm and ability for acting and stage management led to his being nominated to the position of president of the college drama group, and his interest and involvement in college politics led to his becoming president of the student body. Already he was learning to become a leader, and it served to spur him on in every activity in which he participated.

It was while he was at University that his mother taught him a valuable lesson which he never forgot. He'd managed to put by a little money but lost it all in a game of cards. When he confessed to his mother what he'd done, she scolded him and said, 'You're a fool, Issy. Why bet money on cards? What do they know about you? What do they care? If you want to bet, bet on yourself.' It was sound advice, which Issy would always remember.

After four hard years of janitoring, wrestling, acting, debating, scrounging and studying, Issy graduated from St Lawrence in 1939 complete with a bachelor of arts degree, to the delight of Bryna who always knew her boy possessed qualities that would best be served by the American education system.

He was also, as usual, broke.

Eager to pursue acting as a career and undeterred by an abject lack of funds, Issy next proceeded to fulfill his goal, which had been forming in his mind over the past few years, to enter the American Academy of Dramatic Arts in New York. To the average student with a penchant for acting, this would have seemed an unlikely avenue without the necessary finance, but to Issur it was now just another hurdle to attack, as had been St Lawrence.

The secretary of the Academy hardly knew what hit him

when Issur Danielovitch turned up at his office, asking, pleading, virtually demanding a scholarship. They had no scholarships available, the secretary explained. Issy was adamant. He refused to accept that they would not admit him on a mere technicality, and he gave them all the reasons under the sun as to why they should find room for him. He sold himself hook, line and sinker. He persuaded the Academy to give him an audition and presented the board with a dynamic performance. He displayed his persuasive enthusiasm which seemed inexhaustible, and it was sufficient to convince the Academy to make an exception and create a special scholarship just for him.

Now enrolled at the Academy, Issy set about seeking employment and living quarters. He turned up at the settlement house in Greenwich village and struck a bargain there. He would be given a room and meals at the house in return for his services. He would teach the children at the settlement house all about drama, and so even while he was training as an actor, he was already teaching others all he so far knew about the art of acting. Issy still needed to earn himself some pocket money, and he took dozens of other part-time jobs. He was a professional wrestler, an usher, a parking-lot attendant, a bell-hop, and a soda jerk nearly every evening at Schrafft's restaurant.

It was at the American Academy of Arts that Issy met and fell in love with classmate Diana Dill from Bermuda. Another classmate was one Betty Pepske who later, as Lauren Bacall, would have a hand in Issy's future.

It was about this time that Issy decided to change his name. He was appearing in summer stock theatres and, to his delight, getting paid for it. It was during a summer stock season that he made up his mind to take upon himself a professional name. Douglas seemed a good idea. It had certainly done no harm to swashbuckling screen star Douglas Fairbanks Senior. So Douglas became his surname. He dreamed up Kirk himself, thinking it had a 'snazzy' ring to it.

Kirk Douglas graduated from the American Academy of Dramatic Arts in 1941, and set his sights on Broadway. With his usual air of almost defiant determination, he landed an interview with Broadway producer Guthrie McClintic.

'Can you sing?' McClintic asked him.

'I can, but not very well,' admitted Kirk, wondering where this line of conversation was going to lead him.

'Well, can you sing loud?' asked McClintic.

'Of course I can,' replied Kirk, deciding on a more positive course of answers.

McClintic handed Kirk a sheet of paper with the words to 'Yankee Doodle' written on it.

'Learn this!' said McClintic.

Many things suddenly passed through Kirk's mind: four years at University struggling to pay his way; two years at the American Academy of Dramatic Arts, paying his way by taking every menial job he could find; studying Greek tragedies, French comedies and the Shakespearean classics. And here he was, making a grand bid for Broadway stardom, and he was having to learn to sing 'Yankee Doodle'! So Kirk went home and learned 'Yankee Doodle' until he knew it forwards, backwards, sideways and inside out. It resulted in his first Broadway appearance . . . playing a singing messengerboy in *Spring Again*. At least he got to watch a legendary actor in action, the star of the show, C. Aubrey Smith

Kirk recalls a time when he was 'bumming around New York' in search of acting jobs and was with a few friends in Central Park. Overlooking the park was a famous hotel, The Hampshire House, an elegant, chic, expensive place.

Kirk turned to one of his pals and said, 'You know something? One day I'm gonna take a suite on the twenty-fifth floor of that hotel and look out over the park and say, "Well, Kirk, you've arrived." ' And with that he opened a bottle of beer and drank it down.

Kirk landed his second Broadway experience in Katherine Cornell's production of *The Three Sisters*. Only he didn't appear in the play. He acted as stage manager and played an off-stage echo from the wings. At least it was a job and even though he didn't get to walk on stage, he was for a time part of an auspicious theatrical company, and on Thanksgiving Day, 1941, he was invited to a supper party thrown by Katherine Cornell at which Kirk got to rub shoulders with the elite of the American Theatre.

It was the last time he would appear with the big names of

Broadway for three years. He received his call-up papers and, leaving Diana Dill and Broadway behind for the sake of Uncle Sam, he dutifully reported for service in the navy. His home for the next year was the midshipman school at Notre Dame University from which he graduated as a naval ensign. His next port of call was much more remote. He was to serve for the most part of 1942 and 1943 patrolling the Pacific Ocean as a communications officer on an anti-submarine patrol craft.

Towards the end of 1943 his unit was involved in an encounter with a Japanese submarine in which Anti-submarine Unit 1139, on which Kirk served, trailed the enemy below, dropping depth charges. The waters were particularly shallow and the charges were set to go off almost as soon as they hit the water. One charge, however, exploded too soon, and Kirk was among the crew members who caught the force of the blast. He suffered serious internal injuries and was immediately admitted to the Balboa Hospital at the San Diego Naval Station. He was in hospital for five months, during which time he was patched up and treated for the additional complication of severe dysentery, caused by his shattered internal system.

Although Kirk was seriously ill and permanently out of the war, he and Diana took the opportunity to get married, and on 2 November 1943 Miss Dill became Diana Douglas. Following Kirk's discharge from the navy in 1944, the Douglases returned to New York where both hoped to resume their careers on the stage.

THREE/Champion

Kirk Douglas landed his first major professional acting role on the New York stage in *Kiss and Tell*. In this he succeeded another newcomer who had made his debut in the play just a year earlier—Richard Widmark. Douglas quickly became an actor of some reputation, and on the strength of *Kiss and Tell*, he successively played in *Trio*, *Star In The Window* and, most noticeably, *Alice In Arms*, in which he received his first really fine notices for his role of an army sergeant.

At home life was blossoming. Diana had given up her career when she became pregnant. Their first son, Michael, was born on 25 September 1944. To be a father filled Kirk with pride and some trepidation. He was determined not to be the kind of father his own had been.

One of the great training grounds for actors in the late Forties was radio. Most of the actors who made it big in movies in the Fifties, such as Douglas, and have survived to become what we now term as 'veterans', did a lot of ground work in radio. Kirk, eager for experience and money, accepted roles in a number of radio soap operas. These long preceded the television soap operas which are so prevalent in the United States today and which, like radio before, allow hundreds of American newcomers the opportunity to practise their craft professionally. Radio, however, is something which Kirk believes had its advantages because it relied totally on the voice and therefore gave actors a unique kind of training.

Kirk was rehearsing to play the Unknown Soldier in the play *The Wind Is Ninety* when he received a surprise visitor. It was Hollywood producer Hal B. Wallis from Paramount Studios. He was in New York on business and wanted to see Kirk Douglas in action on the advice of Kirk's former AADA classmate, Lauren Bacall, who was at this time just starting out in movies. She had seen Kirk at work and believed he had a special magic that simply called out to be exploited by the cinema screen. Kirk was astounded when Hal Wallis offered him a movie contract.

Kirk Douglas told me, 'At the beginning of my career I never saw myself as a movie actor. The first time Hal Wallis saw me in a play and offered me a part in a movie, I turned it down because I was embarrassed. I never thought of myself as a *movie* actor. I thought they had to be someone at the top.' So, incredibly, Kirk turned the offer down and went on to score a big hit opposite Wendell Corey, Bert Lytell and Blanche Yurka in *The Wind Is Ninety*. Then the play closed and Kirk was stuck for another play to do.

'It wasn't until the play closed and another play didn't materialize and I was broke, married and needed some money that I thought, gee, I wonder if that feller from Hollywood still wants me,' said Kirk. 'So I called California, and the next thing I knew was I was on my way out there.'

Wallis was enthusiastic about his new discovery and arranged for Paramount to fly Douglas out to Hollywood and give him a screen test for a role in *The Strange Loves Of Martha Ivers* opposite Barbara Stanwyck. Considering the popular image of the tough, aggressive Kirk Douglas that everybody would come to either love or hate, Kirk won the role of a rather weak-willed character. Stanwyck played the kind of super-bitch that would decades later make Joan Collins an international star. Stanwyck's character, Martha Ivers, was, at the tender age of thirteen, responsible for the death of her aunt. She succeeds in escaping discovery while an innocent man is sent to the gallows for the murder. Martha's young boyfriend (Van Heflin), whom she assumes witnessed the killing, leaves town but returns years later as a gambler. By now Martha is a rich, powerful lady who virtually runs the small American town where she lives.

This is where Kirk Douglas comes in as a lad, now grown up, who did see Martha kill her aunt. He marries Martha and becomes the local district attorney, but in reality he is just a pawn for the ruthless Martha. When Heflin returns, they assume he is going to blackmail them. In fact, he knows nothing of the murder, but when he does discover the truth, he threatens to blackmail them, causing Martha to use her womanly ways on him. Then she tries to persuade Heflin to murder Douglas.

It was a prestigious melodrama with which to start Kirk off as a screen actor. The film was tautly directed by Lewis Milestone who had previously enjoyed many successes such as *All Quiet On The Western Front*, *The Front Page*, *The General Died At Dawn* and, immediately before *Martha Ivers*, *A Walk In The Sun*. To have Barbara Stanwyck as a leading lady was a coup for Douglas considering this was his first film. She was, during the Forties, at the height of her career and *Martha Ivers* is generally considered one of her best movies of the decade. Unhappily, her career faded somewhat in the Fifties. However, at this time, if any actress could dominate Douglas in a movie it was Queen Vixen herself Barbara Stanwyck, who still looked fabulous even though she was almost ten years older than Kirk.

With the success of *Martha Ivers* Wallis and Paramount were eager to have their new boy succeed his 1946 movie debut with an immediate follow-up picture. Their boy, however, had other ideas. He saw himself as a stage actor who'd made a movie because he needed the money. 'I did the film and right after that I went back to Broadway to do another play,' he told me. 'That play lasted about two or three nights. So . . . !'

The short-running play was *Woman Bites Dog*, and following that times were lean again. It was 1947, and Diana had given birth to another son, Joel, on 23 January. With a wife, two children and no work on his mind, Kirk again began thinking about movies. He called Paramount in Hollywood, and as before Hal Wallis was pleased to see his new discovery willing to give films another go. This time Kirk submitted to a contract with Wallis at Paramount, starting at 500 dollars a week.

Somebody at Paramount must have taken a close look at him and decided he wasn't your average-looking leading man with that prominent dimple stuck on his chin. It was decided that it needed to be filled in. But Kirk got so mad about it, he told them, 'If you don't like the hole in the chin, I'm going back to Broadway.' They left the chin alone. Kirk has always liked the look of his face. He describes it as 'aggressive-looking, interesting, not handsome, but certainly not ugly'.

Now hooked on the idea of being a movie actor, Kirk gave his mother a phone call with the exciting news of his contract.

'Ma, I'm under contract to Hal B. Wallis for 500 dollars a week,' he told her.

'Yes, son,' she replied, 'but are you having enough to eat?'

After all the initial excitement, Wallis now had nothing to put Kirk into, so he hired him out to RKO to do *Out Of The Past*. It was an important break for Kirk. It was only his second movie, yet he was given the second male lead, the first male lead going to Robert Mitchum, who was a year younger than Kirk but had been making movies since 1943. Mitchum, who was just a year away from being convicted for smoking marijuana cigarettes and a two-month jail sentence, played a laconic private eye who wants to retire. Douglas played the kind of charming son-of-a-bitch at which he excels. In this case he was a hoodlum who discovers an unfortunate slant to Mitchum's past and blackmails him into doing a shady job for him.

The two leading ladies in the film were Jane Greer, one of RKO's major stars who played a beautiful villainess, and Rhonda Fleming, a ravishing redhead, who became a firm friend of Kirk in real life, as did Mitchum.

At this early stage of his career Kirk Douglas was pretty much tossed to and fro as the waves carried him. If he had then enjoyed the kind of control over his own work he would later fight for, he would undoubtedly have steered a course away from the RKO studios who were eager to retain him for a further picture which would prove to be a classic Hollywood disaster.

RKO planned, produced and released *Mourning Becomes Electra* as a blockbuster. Dudley Nichols, the noted screenplaywright, wrote, produced and directed this marathon screen adaptation of Eugene O'Neill's play, whittling the original stage version down from six hours to three hours of screen time. This was only Nichols's third directorial effort. It was also his last. Kirk Douglas was suddenly relegated somewhat by RKO to sixth billing, although every actor billed above him was someone of note. There was Rosalind Russell, Michael Redgrave, Raymond Massey, Katina Paxinou and Leo Genn.

RKO had expected *Mourning Becomes Electra* to be their *Gone With The Wind*, since it was set during the days of the American Civil War. However, it was far more intellectual and, although this was by far the most ambitious and expensive motion picture which RKO had ever attempted, their limited resources dictated that the film be shot in black and white.

It had always been considered a rather daring play to transfer to the screen. Various major studios had considered filming it, but it had always been rejected. It was considered uncommercial and very costly. Dudley Nichols, however, greatly admired the play and envisioned it as a prestigious motion picture on an epic scale but with greater character dimension than the usual costume melodrama. He succeeded in getting O'Neill's personal approval to write a screenplay which he showed to Rosalind Russell and Raymond Massey. Both stars were eager to do the film if it could be launched, and so with O'Neill's blessing and a firm commitment from two of Hollywood's most important stars of the Forties, Nichols was able to persuade RKO to produce *Mourning Becomes Electra*.

It had the kind of plot that makes even *Dallas* look tame. The Mannons are nineteenth-century Ewings. Rosalind Russell played a sort of female JR who falls in love with her mother's lover and persuades her weak-willed brother, played by Redgrave, to kill their mother's boyfriend. The mother has already murdered her husband, and eventually Russell drives her mother to suicide. Somewhere amongst all this, Kirk Douglas turns up as a young army officer who falls in love with Russell, which is his misfortune.

The film was first released as a road-show prestige picture with an intermission, just like *Gone With The Wind* eight years earlier. But audiences stayed away and the film finished its initial release with twenty-five minutes cut out. Actually, the critics quite liked the film, but it went far over the heads of the filmgoers of 1947. By the time it was generally released, a further twenty minutes had been cut. In its original form, *Mourning Becomes Electa* was powerful stuff, but it was certainly a picture which Kirk Douglas could have done without. It did

29

nothing for him, and he was unable to offer much to his one-dimensional role.

That same year, 1947, Kirk first met and worked with an actor whose career had followed much the same path as Kirk's, and with whom Douglas would enjoy a long friendship and professional association—Burt Lancaster. Both Lancaster and Douglas had been plucked from Broadway by Hal B. Wallis in 1946, and as Lancaster once noted, 'We both came from sort of humble beginnings. We were both young, brash, cocky, arrogant. We knew everything, were highly opinionated. We were invincible. Nobody liked us.' Sheilah Graham, the Hollywood gossip columnist, tagged the stars as 'The Terrible-Tempered Twins'. Their tempers were certainly ignited during the making of *I Walk Alone*. There were numerous arguments with Wallis about their roles, which neither actor particularly relished. They played a pair of bootleg racketeers, and neither part could boast any redeeming qualities, although Lancaster's character did manage to win some sympathy but only because Douglas proved thoroughly despicable when he double-crosses his partner.

Not only did they hate their roles, but they also complained that they were grossly underpaid considering the following each had quickly acquired among cinema-goers. But what really needled Kirk was that he saw all too plainly how he was being type-cast in a villainous mould. His role in *I Walk Alone* was easily comparable to his part in *Out Of The Past*. The terrible twins were quickly earning for themselves unenviable reputations for being difficult. Somehow Lancaster would succeed in living down this image, but for Douglas it would be something he would never quite be able to shake off.

For now, though, he was more concerned about his work than his image. He wanted something done, and he decided that since nobody else was going to do it, he would. His contract with Wallis called for five films. So far he had made only one for his employer. One was enough, he decided, and broke his contract. He was suddenly freelance which, except for a brief period in the near future, would set the pattern for the rest of his career. He was told that no one succeeded without a studio contract, but he was adamant. It meant that for a while he would not have it all his own way, but he was content to bide his time, waiting for the right picture to come along at the right time which, he hoped, would put him in a league where contracts would be totally unnecessary. He was fast proving to be one of Hollywood's most reckless gamblers. When I once asked him about his success as a gambler, he said, 'Every movie I make is a gamble. At best this is a precarious profession. Making movies is not a steady job where you start at nine o'clock in the morning and work through until five every day. When one movie is over, you're out of a job.'

Out of work, but eager to press on, Kirk accepted, more out of a need to work than anything else, an offer from 20th Century-Fox to appear in *The Walls Of Jericho*. The film hardly offered Kirk any kind of challenge except to survive a star vehicle designed purely for Cornel Wilde and Linda Darnell. Even Anne Baxter was playing second fiddle in this soap opera. The picture had been manufactured by Fox to reunite Wilde and Darnell who had scored a huge box office success together in the costume drama *Forever Amber*. Kirk Douglas was simply there to play Wilde's best friend. It was at least something of a relief from playing sons-of-bitches.

Like most dramatic actors, Kirk had a hankering to do comedy. Unfortunately, few movie makers saw Kirk Douglas as a laughter maker and so the best comedy scripts never got around to him. They were always snapped up by Cary Grant. However, when the script for *My Dear Secretary* came Kirk's way, he saw his chance to show everyone that he could do more than make people hate him. His leading lady was Laraine Day, a devout Mormon descended from a prominent Mormon pioneer leader. She had gained much popularity when she appeared as Nurse Mary Lamont in *Dr Kildare* at MGM, and because of her beliefs her films were generally clean-cut and free from the kind of sordid characters which Douglas was used to playing. She and Kirk actually made a joyful combination, and the film led to Kirk landing a role in that same year, 1948, in another comedy, *A Letter To Three Wives*.

It was the clever, witty tale of three wives who each receive a letter from a mysterious woman whom we never see, stating that she is about to run off with one of their husbands. Each wife then examines her life and marriage, wondering if hers is the husband in question. The three wives were played by Jeanne

Crain, Linda Darnell and Ann Southern. Kirk played Southern's husband. In one scene Ann returns home believing her husband is up to no good but is delightfully surprised to find him alone at home. Director Joseph L. Mankiewicz wanted Ann Southern to react in a particular way that expressed both her surprise and delight. While preparing for this scene, Mankiewicz took Kirk aside and the two hatched a secret plot. Mankiewicz suggested to Kirk that, without Ann knowing it, he strip down to his underpants and hide behind the sofa situated on the living-room set. Then when Ann came in, he was to leap up. Mankiewicz believed the results on Ann's face would be just what he wanted from her.

Kirk eagerly complied and while Ann was taken off to one side of the set, Kirk took off his trousers and shirt and ducked down behind the sofa. Mankiewicz called for rehearsal, and Ann began the sequence. She came through the door and Kirk leapt to his feet. Ann displayed the reaction that Mankiewicz had been aiming for. Thereafter, Ann Southern was able to produce that same element of amazement in each subsequent rehearsal, through to the actual 'take'.

Kirk enjoyed working with Mankiewicz immensely. The legendary director had supplied Kirk with his first totally likeable and wholly believable film role. The film was also a triumph for Mankiewicz who won two Oscars, one for his screenplay and one for his direction.

Mankiewicz was aware that Douglas was looking to become something more than just another Hollywood leading man. He even became something of a confidant to Kirk during the making of *A Letter To Three Wives* when Kirk showed Mankiewicz a script he had read called *Champion*. It was the story of a most unscrupulous boxer which producer Stanley Kramer had offered to him. Douglas was fascinated by the role but was uncertain about whether he could, or should, do it. Kramer was at that time virtually unknown and had not yet started directing his own movies. He had produced only three previous pictures through his independent film company, Screen Plays Inc., but even though his films were modestly budgeted they were bursting with quality. The screenplay of *Champion*, by Carl Foreman, was brilliant. Kramer had gone to Douglas, offering him the star role but not a star's salary. The budget for the film was limited to just half a million dollars and Kirk's fee would be fifteen thousand bucks.

His agent was thunderstruck to learn that Kirk was thinking of taking Foreman's offer when MGM were willing to pay Douglas a staggering fifty thousand dollar fee, by far the most he'd ever been offered for a single role, to play a supporting part opposite Gregory Peck and Ava Gardner in *The Great Sinner*. Go with MGM, the agent urged Kirk. But Kirk felt his gambler instinct telling him to go with Kramer. His agent told Kirk he was out of his mind. Out of it or in it, Kirk's mind was made up. In preparation for his role, he took boxing lessons so that he would at least look as though he could handle himself in the ring. This type of preparation set a precedent for Douglas who would continue to take great pains in ensuring that his actions in motion pictures would look authentic. The gamble paid off. Released in 1949, *Champion* was a knock-out at the box office and Kirk was nominated for a Best Actor Academy Award. The film also served to seal the tough-guy image upon Kirk that he's never been quite able to shake off.

It was an image that put him on the line in certain situations, and he quickly learned how to handle it, but not in a way that could possibly be accused of feeding that image. In fact, one particular incident almost succeeded in destroying his image yet enforced his reputation for being among the most quick-witted actors in the business. It was late one night when *Champion* was still pulling 'em in that Kirk stepped into a Los Angeles bar for a quick drink. From a group of drinkers stepped a rather large and very drunk man who eyed Douglas, recognizing the actor who'd been so tough as a boxer on the screen. He ambled over to Kirk and without a word drove his fist into that famous dimpled chin. The whole place suddenly fell silent.

All eyes were on Kirk, the Champ, waiting for him to retaliate. It promised to be a fight greater than any featured in *Champion*.

But Kirk was to disappoint the eager crowd.

He stood against the bar and shouted, 'Anyone in this bar can lick me.'

The drunk staggered back with a puzzled look on his face. He seemed to be trying to figure this one out. This movie star who was so tough on the screen just had no inclination to prove himself and even admitted that he wasn't up to a fight. Then with confusion reigning in his head, the drunk slunk back to his table and Kirk finished his drink with no further interruptions.

While Kirk's career was rising rapidly, he was conscious of his role at home, and took his father's example as being one to avoid at all costs. As a father, he was in his element and he now enjoyed the kind of family togetherness which had so cruelly eluded his own childhood years. His own parents had been reunited, but as far as Herschel was concerned, Kirk was unable to completely forgive or forget. But he adored his mother and told her, 'One day I'm going to put your name up in lights.' She just laughed, but it was a promise he would keep.

Herschel, however, failed completely to win his son over. Kirk would have loved for his father to just make the effort, but the old man never could bring himself to express love and pride in his son's achievements. Once Herschel came to Kirk and asked for a loan. Kirk was furious that his father should even think of asking him for a favour. 'No!' he yelled. 'What the hell have you ever done for me? All I ever wanted was a pat on the back.' Herschel just stayed silent, unable to express his emotions, if indeed he had any.

His memories marred by his father's coldness, Kirk made every exacting effort to go the other way with his own sons. He praised them for any little thing that they accomplished, whether it was eating with a spoon for the first time, or taking that first precarious step. And he was seeing to it that his boys would not have to go without.

But life in the Douglas household was not all roses. Diana had given up her career to be a wife and mother and was beginning to feel trapped by her domestic responsibilities. She yearned to carve out a career of her own. She watched her husband steaming full speed ahead in Hollywood while she had to come to terms with the fact that she was being left far behind.

In fact, it would have been difficult for anyone to keep up with Kirk Douglas. After *Champion* he had become *the* big new star and every studio was after him, waving contracts. 20th Century-Fox bosses were kicking themselves because they had decided not to take up the option for a second film from Douglas after *A Letter To Three Wives*, and they now offered him 200,000 dollars to portray Field Marshal Rommel in a picture they were planning.

It is said that it was at this time that the Kirk Douglas we've all come to know, though not necessarily love, was born. He was quickly learning the business end of the market, and he was enjoying the luxury of sifting through the offers coming his way. And all the time he had this idea in his mind that someday he'd want to be the one who pulls the strings. The aggression was becoming predominant.

It was also at this time that Kirk and Diana decided to go their separate ways, declaring that their differences stemmed from career conflicts. With Diana went the two boys, but at least there was no bitterness, at least none that was long-lasting between Kirk and Diana, and the time would come when the two would even work together on a picture.

Still the offers came pouring in. Kirk had already broken one contract, but now he felt that perhaps he could afford to go along with the system for a time, knowing that eventually he would beat it anyway, and so he settled for a seven-year contract with Warner Bros. But he ensured that it allowed him to do one film outside of the studio per year, so in essence he was not tied down solely to any one studio.

Now that he was a big name in town, he used it to champion a cause. He joined hundreds of other Hollywood names in opposing the terrible witch-hunt that had been in progress in the movie capital. The House Un-American Activities Committee was immersed in rooting out communist infiltrators within the industry, and a number of prominent people in the business would be blacklisted. However, John Huston, Philip Dunne, William Wyler and Alexander Knox got together to form the Committee for the First Amendment to put forward the case for freedom in religion, speech and politics. About five hundred others joined them, including Douglas, Burt Lancaster, Danny Kaye, Humphrey Bogart, Lauren Bacall, Henry Fonda, Gregory Peck, Paulette Goddard, Joseph Cotten, Katherine Hepburn and Gene Kelly.

The Committee for the First Amendment was quickly labelled as a communist front organization, which was rubbish. To take Kirk Douglas's case alone is enough to prove the point. As a Jew, and with the background from which he came, Douglas had no sympathy with communists. In fact, he told me, 'I've seen how grey things are in communist countries. I've seen how unhappy people are. I think our democratic system gives you more of a chance. Even with our faults, and in recent years we've certainly seen them, I still believe it's the best system. The only thing is, it's got to get better.'

Now that Kirk was separated from his wife, he began dating other women. One of his dates was Rhonda Fleming, whom he took one night to a big Hollywood party thrown by agent and producer Charlie Feldman at the Crescendo nightclub in Los Angeles. Fleming sat on one side of him, and on the other side sat actress Evelyn Keyes whose date was Farley Granger. When Evelyn saw Kirk, she was smitten. Determined to capture his interest, she turned on all the charm and sexuality she could muster. Kirk may have come to the party with Rhonda Fleming, but when he left he had only one woman on his mind, Evelyn Keyes. They began a passionate affair which lasted for four months, but there was more to their relationship than just being lovers. They had become very close friends, and remained so for years after their fling was over.

Kirk now had fame and wealth, but he was not a fulfilled man. The breakdown of his marriage had rocked him, and although his career was blossoming, he felt he was lacking in some secret ingredient—something that would mean more to him than material wealth. He wanted emotional stability. His anxieties and frustrations eventually led him to the inevitable psychoanalyst's couch where so many of Hollywood's elite find themselves when the tinsel and glamour of the movie mecca begins to blot out the harsh realities of the real world which still manage to infiltrate seemingly secure lives.

Often before going to his appointments with the analyst, Kirk would turn up at Evelyn Keyes's apartment. He would put his problems to her and expect to get some of the answers to his questions. Then he'd continue on to the analyst where he would present everything that Evelyn had said, comparing them with the doctor's answers. Then he'd return to Evelyn's place and tell her whether or not the doctor agreed with her prognosis. She would then proceed, at Kirk's prompting, to express her opinion on whatever the analyst had said. For hours on end, Kirk would pace up and down on her living-room floor like an expectant father. Sometimes he did his pacing in the bedroom.

One day he expressed to her his concerns over what the House Un-American Activities Committee was doing, and he told Evelyn that if he were to win the Oscar for *Champion*, he would take the opportunity to tell everyone how he felt about the dreadful witch-hunt.

As fate would have it, Kirk didn't win the Oscar. He was bitterly disappointed. But instead of mooning over the fact, he got back to work, intent on making his life and career as satisfying as he had always dreamed it might be someday.

But Kirk still had self-doubts. His anxieties reached a pinnacle one day when he visited New York and fulfilled an ambition which he had long dreamed of. In the end it meant nothing. As he had once promised, he checked in at the famous Hampshire House Hotel. And as he had boasted to his friends, he took a suite on the twenty-fifth floor and ordered a bottle of champagne. Looking out over Central Park, Kirk opened the champagne and drank.

'And then something strange happened,' he recalls. 'The elation I thought I'd feel turned to a hollow anticlimax. I felt desperately sad. I'd got to what I wanted, so where did I go from there?

'I decided to go inside myself to look for a point of view—a philosophy to my life. The most important thing for me after so many years of struggle was to learn how to cope with my success and not let it destroy me, as it has destroyed so many people.'

Perhaps that is why Kirk Douglas has been a champion for so long.

FOUR /
/The Big Cheese

It didn't take too long for Kirk to realize that he had made a mistake in signing a contract with Warner Bros. It wasn't the studio which he disliked—just the system. At least, he knew it wasn't right for him. In fact, he was not totally against the star system, contrary to popular belief. Kirk is often considered as Hollywood's first rebel—at least, the first rebel who succeeded. The truth is, Kirk Douglas simply rejects that which is not right for him. He believed, and rightly so, that he could do much more to further his own career without the limitations which a studio contract then dictated.

But ask him, as I did, if he was totally against the system, and he'd reply, 'Not at all. I think there are a lot of tremendous advantages to working under a studio. I even used to be a little envious of that. Sometimes!

'It gave actors a home base. The studio would try hard to get their people parts to play and I think the studios did a lot of good things. They gave a lot of young people small parts on a small salary, and they'd develop them. They had training programmes like dancing and singing and learning to fight so it looked real on the screen.'

Kirk's contract with Warners lasted just two years, and in that time he was able to see exactly where he was heading. They were turning him into an average leading man, an ordinary kind of screen hero, and as Kirk once said, 'I never was an *ordinary* guy!' True, he could have continued to churn out

38

regular performances and make a good living at it. But Kirk wanted more than just money from his work. He was looking for the kind of satisfaction that only intensely challenging roles could offer. And that he did later achieve, but for the time being while he was under contract to Warners, it was not easy.

Certainly the association with Warners started off promisingly in 1950 with *Young Man With A Horn*. It was based on a novel by Dorothy Baker who used as her inspiration the life of Bix Beiderbecke, an American jazz legend. Warner Bros had bought the screen rights to the novel back in 1945 but had shelved the project while they searched for a suitable actor who could portray the compulsive but sensitive musician, Rick Martin, who was based very much on Bix Beiderbecke.

Kirk Douglas, fresh from his success in *Champion* and now under contract to Warners, seemed the ideal choice. And *Young Man With A Horn* seemed an ideal star vehicle for their latest acquisition. They also had Doris Day and decided the film would give her ample opportunity to stage several musical numbers. But the key element of the film was the trumpet work. Up to this time Kirk had never so much as picked up a trumpet, let alone played one. But with his usual almost obsessive zeal, he studied playing trumpet under Larry Sullivan, the studio's own trumpet player, who performed as a member of their orchestra on the soundtrack of hundreds of pictures. Kirk spent three months learning to play the trumpet, and after that time he not only was able to finger the valves correctly and purse his lips to the mouthpiece like an expert, but he could also play the instrument after a certain fashion. So delighted was he with his new-found talent that he used to sit in his dressing-room between scenes playing the horn until finally director Michael Curtiz had to ask him to stop it because he was disturbing the whole company.

Kirk was delighted to have Lauren Bacall in the picture as well, since it was her recommendation to Hal Wallis that introduced Douglas to the movies. Hoagy Carmichael, who had known Bix Beiderbecke personally, was also cast as a sort of on-screen narrator as well as being Douglas's on-screen best friend in the picture.

The results, handled under the disciplined eye of Hungarian director Michael Curtiz, were certainly very good, and Kirk was particularly convincing both in his acting and his trumpet playing. Warners wasted no time in casting Kirk in his second movie for them, *The Glass Menagerie*. The script, by Peter Berneis and Tennessee Williams, based on Williams's own play, certainly attracted Kirk, and he was feeling that perhaps he could function in quality films and still be under contract. Technically, the film was a success, but commercially it just didn't have enough going for it, and Kirk was disappointed with the results.

Initially Kirk had been able to feel that Warners were attempting to find him quality subjects with challenging roles, but the shape of things to come began to form with Kirk's next picture for Warners, *Along The Great Divide*. It was Kirk's first excursion into the Wild West, and although he was being directed by the veteran of many other westerns, Raoul Walsh, it was purely B-feature material in terms of story line. Kirk was the new but dutiful Marshal who has to bring in Walter Brennan who's accused of murder. However, by the time they have made the perilous journey across deserts and mountains, the Marshal comes to realize that the old man is innocent and guns down the real villain. Also along for the ride was beautiful Virginia Mayo as Brennan's daughter with whom Kirk inevitably rides off into the sunset.

Although none too enthusiastic about the script, Kirk was excited about making his first western, and he set about learning to ride a horse and handle six shooters. For the first time he also had the exhilarating experience of filming out on location under clear blue skies. Walsh took his company up in the High Sierras and around Lone Pine in California, and then to the stark Mojave desert.

Hooked on the idea of doing more worthy westerns at some time, Kirk was distinctly unimpressed with the script Warners next offered to him, *The Big Trees*, another western only far inferior to even *Along The Great Divide*. Before that, however, he enjoyed some breathing space and made two of his very finest films, *Ace In The Hole* and *Detective Story*, both for Paramount. Both these pictures were the kind Kirk was looking for that offered him challenges as an actor to which he had not yet been exposed. And he had two first-rate directors to help him through the experiences.

Billy Wilder had written his own script based on a true incident when a miner was trapped for days in a collapsed mine. He also produced and directed *Ace In The Hole*, as it came to be called, and cast Kirk in the difficult role of a cynical reporter who uses the disaster to create his own very special newspaper story. Controlling the overall press coverage and the rescue operation, he becomes a paper hero who in fact delays the rescue operation so long that the trapped victim finally dies.

By now something else was eating at Kirk in his relentless pursuit of the perfect star vehicle. He had become increasingly concerned about all aspects of the pictures he was making, and *Ace In The Hole* was a picture he particularly cared about. He was also constantly on the lookout for first-class roles and seemed obsessed with considering every film role that was available to him or anybody else. Noting this aspect of Kirk's nature one day on the set of *Ace In The Hole*, Billy Wilder said to him, 'Kirk, you remind me of the old Austrian story about the man who committed suicide because he couldn't dance at two weddings at the same time!'

Kirk's performance was brilliant, and Wilder produced a technically and artistically exemplary motion picture. There was just one snag, which Wilder, Douglas and Paramount seemed to have overlooked. The press, who came to review the film, were not impressed with the way they were portrayed in the picture. Also, by 1951 standards, it was too harrowing a movie to be considered entertaining, and the public could not be enticed. Paramount, desperate for publicity and favourable reviews, tried to soothe the press and even changed the title to *The Big Carnival*, but sadly the film was a box office flop. It has, however, grown over the years into a classic and is often studied by young film students, and it always gets a showing whenever a retrospective of either Douglas or Wilder is presented.

Detective Story, directed by William Wyler, offered a different kind of challenge. It had already played successfully on the stage, for which it was written by Sidney Kingley. What fascinated Kirk was Wyler's courageous and successful attempt to transfer the play to the screen without radically changing the physical setting, which was a New York police station. With the exception of one scene in a police vehicle, the film managed to remain within the confines of the police station without making it look like a filmed stage play. Kirk was also hooked on the part itself, that of a fanatical detective, dedicated to justice but brutal in his methods. To prepare himself, and determined to bring an air of authenticity to the part, Kirk spent about seven days and nights at the 16th Precinct in New York, observing the policemen at work, the visitors with complaints, the criminals brought in, and just generally breathing in the atmosphere.

He was also delighted to learn that Wyler was hiring many of the actors who had appeared in the original New York stage production of *Detective Story*. Eager to get the most out of this play and the role, Kirk asked William Wyler and the associate producer Willie Schorr if it could be arranged for the play to be staged at the Sombrero Playhouse in Phoenix, Arizona with all the film's cast playing their respective characters. It was duly arranged, and Kirk found himself back on a real stage doing a play for the first time in almost five years. More importantly, it gave him, and the rest of the cast, an opportunity to rehearse out the whole film in an unconventional but productive manner. It also led to the film being made in just five weeks, the shortest time it had ever taken Wyler, who was always meticulous in exploring every facet and detail of every scene, to make a picture.

In contrast to the stories of Kirk's temperament and difficult behaviour that would later emerge, William Wyler, surely one of the cinema's toughest directors, is on record as saying that his association with Kirk Douglas 'was the best star-director relationship I ever had'.

Kirk was understandably proud of his performance in *Detective Story*, but he was bitterly disappointed not to receive the recognition he certainly deserved for his performance from the Academy Of Motion Picture Arts and Sciences. 'I thought that performance was Oscar calibre,' he muses, 'but I didn't even get nominated.'

By now Kirk was thoroughly disillusioned with Warner Bros and the material they were offering him. *The Big Trees* was the last straw. One reviewer aptly retitled it, *The Big Cheese*. So despondent was Kirk, and so eager was he to break away from Warners that he offered to make the film for nothing if, after it was in the can, they would release him from his contract. The studio agreed, and so Kirk made his last film under contract and the result was a poor action adventure filmed on location in northern California, but with stock footage from the 1938 production *Valley Of The Giants* inter-cut with the new footage.

Although totally unenthusiastic about the picture, Kirk made every effort to make his performance convincing, and after it was released in 1952 he loyally defended it, saying that it was a picture to please youngsters, that it was a good piece of commercial entertainment. However, years later he would admit, '*The Big Trees*—I hated that film. The trouble is, everywhere I go, it's playing on TV!'

Since 1952 Kirk has never worked under contract, and it would be only a few more years before he would be working for himself.

In the meantime, he still had to earn a living, and his next picture was one he particularly enjoyed making. It was Howard Hawks's sprawling western, or to be more accurate, American period piece, *The Big Sky*. It told the story of a keelboat expedition to establish a new trading-post in 1830. Douglas played a happy-go-lucky trapper whose young companion, Dewey Martin, looks up to him. There is some romantic interest along the hard voyage into the wild lands of the northwest when they pick up a passenger, an Indian princess played by Elizabeth Threatt. But the mainstay of the story is the relationship between Martin and his substitute brother, Douglas.

Howard Hawks not only directed *The Big Sky* but personally produced it as well. And he purposely hired only one major star, which was Douglas. Certainly, Kirk was enough for Hawks, a true veteran, to handle. Douglas couldn't help but come up with ideas which he felt would change and improve elements. Hawks was able to maintain control without alienating his star.

The Big Sky, after the depression of *The Big Trees*, rejuvenated Kirk's excitement for making outdoors adventures, and he enjoyed filming in the gorgeous location of the Grand Teton National Park. But as always he yearned for the mankiller parts. Such a role was that of Jonathan Shields, a hard, merciless movie producer who ruthlessly makes his way in Hollywood. This part in the MGM classic *The Bad And The Beautiful* could have been tailor-made for Douglas, although initially

MGM's head of production, Dory Schary, underestimated both the potential of the role and Kirk's subtle talent.

Schary was keen to have director Vincente Minnelli work for the studio, having just made a certain hit for them, *An American In Paris*. MGM now wanted a similar kind of picture from Minnelli and offered him *Lili*. But Minnelli turned it down specifically because it was no different from the picture he'd just finished.

John Houseman, a producer at Metro, also wanted to work with Minnelli, and offered him the task of directing a western, *Tribute To A Bad Man*. But Minnelli was still unimpressed.

In desperation, Schary asked Minnelli just what it was he would like to do.

Minnelli had read a script that had been kicking around the studio for some time. It was *The Bad And The Beautiful*. He announced to Dory Schary that he wanted to do that picture.

'You really want to do that?' asked Schary unbelievingly. 'But that's the story of an out-and-out heel.'

Minnelli disagreed. 'No, I don't think it is,' he said. 'I think anybody like Jonathan Shields who has the charm to get people to work for him and get involved with him must have the charm of the world.'

Schary wanted to know just who Minnelli thought could play such a role. Schary told him, 'Kirk Douglas.'

Minnelli believed that Kirk Douglas was the one actor who could play the role because Shields has strength, but he also has charm, and Douglas was the kind of actor who didn't have to portray strength. It was already there. All Kirk had to do was play completely for charm. The audience, believed Minnelli, knew that the strength was there without Kirk having to prove it.

Minnelli proved to be absolutely correct. Douglas made Shields a man whom you couldn't help but be attracted to yet ultimately wind up detesting. The picture, which bristles with characters that Hollywood folk found hard not to put real names to, remains the finest movie about movies. Louella Parsons, the notorious gossip columnist, found it hard to believe that many of Douglas's scenes were not suggested by events in the life of David O. Selznick. The celebrated cast also included Lana Turner, Dick Powell, Barry Sullivan and Gloria

Graham. The film is often considered to be among Turner's best, but somehow inevitably it is always Kirk Douglas who remains best remembered from the film.

MGM knew they were on to something great, and they rushed the picture into release in January 1953, just in the nick of time for it to qualify for the 1952 Academy Awards. The film earned six well-deserved nominations, but only five actually won. They were for Best Supporting Actress (Gloria Graham); Best Screenplay; Best Cinematography; Best Art Direction/Set Decoration; and Best Costume Design. The only nominee not to win was Kirk Douglas. The Best Actor Oscar went to Gary Cooper.

Although Cooper's laconic, lonely US Marshal in *High Noon* was impressive, with Douglas's ruthless, charming, two-faced movie producer to contend with in the Oscar stakes, it does seem, when comparing performances, somewhat surprising that Cooper's performance could be termed 'best'. It was the second time the Academy had bypassed Kirk, and he was naturally disappointed. Yet maybe at this stage of his career Douglas was already earning enemies. There were undoubtedly those who saw his independence as an actor to be a flagrant and insulting demonstration of his disdain for the star system. Here was this newcomer who wanted to be his own boss while Gary Cooper, a beloved character in Hollywood, had spent some years in limbo, unable to enjoy a really huge success after almost thirty years in the business, and suddenly hitting the mark with *High Noon*.

Certainly Harry Cohn, the head of Columbia, disliked Douglas intensely, and was heard to refer to Kirk with colourful vulgarity. Columbia was the one major studio where Kirk Douglas never made a picture, although they did distribute a couple of his films. *Photoplay*, a now defunct though then influential magazine (not to be confused with the British publication of the same name), felt they had enough evidence to call him 'The Most Hated Man In Hollywood'. Hollywood gossip columnist Sheilah Graham once described him as 'boastful, egotistical, resentful of criticism—if anyone dare give it'.

It's certainly true that Kirk Douglas harbours an ego, as does any actor, and perhaps his is that little bit bigger—some would say a great deal bigger—than most. And he readily admits that he is not the most popular man in tinseltown. But he remains to this day somewhat mystified as to why he should be considered such a difficult person to work with:

> You know, I don't know what has given me this terrific reputation for being awkward. I do all my work beforehand. I study, I come up with ideas. I discuss changes with the director and I fight and argue, but you ask any director like Wyler, Wilder, Minnelli or Hawks and you won't find any of them complaining.
>
> I have never had any trouble with people who *work*. If you ask someone about one of my so-called flare-ups and if they've actually seen one they'll usually say, 'Oh, we heard it from . . .' They were never actually there.
>
> If you were to trace down the rumours it would turn out that they came from somebody who didn't do his job in a certain situation. *That's* when I blow my top.

Whether or not around 1953 there was a conspiracy to topple Kirk from his pinnacle, it is certain that despite such a triumphant performance in *The Bad And The Beautiful* he was suddenly no longer king of the hill. His career hit a decline. He appeared for MGM in the romantic trilogy, *The Story Of Three Loves*, in which he appeared in the final episode entitled 'Equilibrium' opposite the beautiful Italian import, Pier Angeli. But he only got the part because of an accident that befell Angeli.

Being the story of two trapeze artistes, the film called for the stars to perform a little on the trapeze. Pier Angeli began the film with Ricardo Montalban as her leading man. However, Angeli broke her wrist during the shooting of one of the ariel scenes and the film was postponed. Montalban, unable to meet with the new schedule, was replaced by Kirk. With his usual zeal, Kirk set about learning to fly the trapeze, training under a professional trapeze artist. He learned not only how to hold the bar correctly and take-off like a true professional, but he actually learned a few neat tricks and was able to fly the trapeze in full view of the camera.

It was more than just an ego boost for Douglas. He was actually enjoying himself and as time went on performing dangerous stunts became a must for Kirk, who would insist on doing as many of his own stunts as his producers, and insurers, would allow.

Unfortunately, despite his enthusiasm for the film, the three individual stories, each with its own set of stars and director, didn't gell to make an entertaining picture, and the film flopped.

Douglas was eager to accept an offer from Stanley Kramer, who'd put him on the map with *Champion*, to do *The Juggler*. It allowed Kirk for the first time to consciously play a Jew, and he gave a generally moving performance of a survivor from a Nazi concentration camp who, believing he has killed a policeman, goes on the run in Israel. As the title suggests, the character Kirk portrayed was a circus juggler. Determined to be as authentic as possible, Kirk learned how to juggle. He got a kick out of learning to do tricks like this, but the great thrill of making *The Juggler* was filming it entirely in Israel.

Producer Kramer and Kirk Douglas had obviously hoped that *The Juggler* would copy *Champion* in making sweet music at the box office. But the tills kept ominously quiet at cinemas where *The Juggler* showed. His career was definitely in the doldrums. But there was about to be a decidedly upward swing in his private life.

FIVE/An Awful Wedded Husband

In 1953 Kirk decided on a new approach to his ailing career. He opted for an offer to make a French picture, *Act Of Love*, to be directed by a Russian, Anatole Litvak. The fact that this film would allow Kirk to qualify for some tax exemption was certainly attractive. But more than that the producers were willing to let this famous Hollywood star dabble a little in the production side, giving Kirk his first real taste of the behind the scenes work. Unfortunately, the film didn't really come to very much and was another failure. It was another GI-meets-French-dame tale. Douglas of course was the GI and waif-like Dany Robin was the girl. More interesting than the love story unfolding before the cameras was the one taking place behind them, and Kirk was again the star. But this did not include Dany Robin.

Kirk had his eye on another French-speaking girl. She was Belgian-born Anne Buydens, the film's unit publicist who had just divorced Belgian businessman Albert Buydens. The romance did not get off to a very smooth start. In fact, Anne did everything to avoid Kirk. They had met on the set of the film one morning, and that very evening Kirk was on the phone to her, asking her out to dinner at Paris's most exclusive restaurant, the Tour d'Argent. Anne didn't like Kirk Douglas. She had already made up her mind about that, based on her previous experiences and knowledge of movie-set affairs. She'd seen romances between movie stars and crew members and they were always over the moment the picture was finished. She had very firm opinions of male actors. They were all vain and egotistical. As for Kirk Douglas, she had no intention of becoming a toy for this very forward, rather egotistical and arrogant American movie star. In no uncertain terms, she told him, 'I am going to bed early. Goodnight.' Kirk persisted over the next few days and finally she agreed to go out with him but only if other people would come along too. She was avoiding intimacy at all costs.

Kirk was invited to take part in the grand Cirque d'Hiver, a sort of French version of Britain's Royal Variety Show, and Anne was given the assignment to get him to the theatre for the rehearsal by three o'clock. She arrived promptly at his apartment, shortly after which the telephone rang. Kirk answered it, and upon replacing the receiver announced to Anne that rehearsals were running late and he wasn't needed until six. Anne was suddenly in the tricky situation of having to spend the next few hours alone with this man. Resigning herself to the fact, she prepared to repel borders, expecting to be immediately seduced. But to her total surprise, Kirk just sat and talked, asking her questions about her life. He was actually interested in her, and she quickly warmed to him.

That evening she watched him performing at the Cirque d'Hiver, and as she did so she realized that she was falling in love with him. She had been impressed by his gentlemanly behaviour and his interest in just talking to her. She maintains that talking has always remained important to them both. It was, she says, his mind which really attracted him more than his looks. Discovering him actually to be intelligent made her forget that he was a film star.

As filming progressed, she decided that more than anything she wanted to marry Kirk. But Kirk simply never brought up the subject of marriage, nor of her going back with him to America. When the picture was over Kirk flew back to America alone. But he and Anne were not apart for long. He had signed to do a picture in Italy, a sword and sandal epic called *Ulysses* in which he was surrounded by actors of varying nationalities including Anthony Quinn, Silvana Mangano and Rossana Podesta. Kirk made sure that Anne was hired as the unit publicist. The romance continued under the strictest discretion.

Anne was particularly impressed with Kirk's knack at learning languages. In Paris he had learned to speak French, and now he was fast picking up Italian. Still Anne waited to hear from Kirk whether or not he wanted her to go to America with him. But again when the film was in the can, Kirk flew home and Anne went back to work in France.

It was a year after they had first met when Kirk phoned Anne at the Cannes Film Festival and said he wanted her to come to the United States. And she did. But there was still no mention of marriage. She refused to stay with him at his house and insisted on staying in a hotel. She was concerned about what people would say if she lived with him and then it all came to nothing. The weeks went happily by, but Anne was looking more and more towards something more permanent. She decided to set a time limit, reasoning that either he loved her enough to marry her or there was no point in continuing and she might just as well go back to Paris. She even made reservations and started to pack.

Then she confronted Kirk and said, 'Look, you have a lot of work to do, so I'm going home. Perhaps when you next come to Europe I may still be around.'

To her astonishment, Kirk gave no response to this clear and final warning. But the next day he was knocking on her hotel room door. 'I want to talk to you,' he announced.

She allowed him in, thinking that he was simply going to say that his two sons were coming to visit him.

'Will you marry me,' he suddenly asked. 'It's all organized. Saturday, after work, we go to Las Vegas and we get married on Sunday.'

'No,' said Anne. 'We go Saturday, we get married Saturday.'

Kirk conceded, and on 29 May 1954, they were married in Las Vegas. Anne, who was not then fluent in English, had problems repeating the vows after the Justice of the Peace, and to the utter surprise of everyone except Kirk she said, 'I promise to take this man for my awful wedded husband!' Kirk has always joked that Anne's marriage vow was a Freudian slip. Certainly Anne walked into the marriage with her eyes open, well aware that Kirk was subject to moods, just like most actors. But over the years she has learned to handle them.

She soon discovered him to be a very demanding husband, and if he tried to call her and her line was engaged, he would get annoyed. He also became quite furious whenever he needed to talk to her and she was busily engaged in some other activity. But Anne, patient and understanding, quickly learned how to cope, ensuring that theirs would be a marriage to last. At first she suffered some insecurity, knowing the kind of work her husband had to do. As she says, 'How can you be sure he will always come home after making love to Fay Dunaway all day for a film? I look at myself in the mirror and she certainly looks a lot better than I do.

'There will always be a certain amount of jealousy because there will always be pretty girls around, but I suppose it is a matter of trust.

'Our best times are still when we can talk together alone. Discussing our work, the plays we see, our problems, our children and our friends.'

Anne quickly came to an incredible understanding of her volatile husband and his tremendous energy. 'I think it must be the life he had as a boy,' she says, adding with a hint of sarcasm, 'To hear Kirk tell it, he was the poorest, most miserable child that ever lived. I think it would annihilate him to meet someone who was poorer than he says he was; he wouldn't be able to believe it.

'He was reared by his mother and his sisters and as a school-boy he had to work to help support the family. I think part of Kirk's life has been a monstrous effort to prove himself and gain recognition in the eyes of his father. The old man is dead now. He died in 1954, but the pattern was set early, and not even four years of psychoanalysis could alter the drives that began as a desire to prove himself.'

Anne is a tremendously loyal wife who never complains about Kirk, but instead makes humorous observations in her quiet, even-tempered way. She says that living with Kirk is like sitting in a beautiful garden right next to a volcano! She has become patiently accustomed to his hyperactive life. She'll expect him to come home after work to change his clothes, have a quick swim, maybe play some tennis, change his clothes again, make umpteen telephone calls, read a script, run a movie, read the papers, eat dinner like it was going out of style, take her for a walk, make some more phone calls, and go to bed. Then she's not surprised if after an hour he wakes up with an idea, gets up to write it down, wakes her up to tell her about it and, with any luck, go back to sleep.

Something which really impressed Anne about Kirk when they married was his reluctance to splash out money on unnecessary luxuries. He had acquired a great deal of money, but because of his background he never splashed out on anything he really didn't need. Even their first home was a relatively small Hollywood bungalow with just five rooms and one bed. But then if Kirk was saving his money to spend it on anything in particular, it was to form his own company, which he did in 1955 and called it Bryna.

SIX/ Path to Glory

While Kirk was drawing up plans to make his own films, he continued to freelance, so Walt Disney snapped him up for his multi-million-dollar live action adventure, *20,000 Leagues Under The Sea*. The legendary creator of Mickey Mouse had only made a few live-action pictures, and he wanted this, his most ambitious, to be populated with star names.

Kirk was to play the hero of the piece, harpoonist Ned Land. Paul Lucas certainly added some class to the fantasy, and Peter Lorre added some marvellously light-hearted moments. To play the heavy, Captain Nemo, Disney wanted James Mason. Mason, however, was reluctant to lend himself to the project which he naturally thought was going to be little more than a children's film.

Mason had another problem. He wanted top billing. So did Kirk Douglas. The situation was made more complicated by the fact that both Mason and Douglas had the same agent, Ray Stark. Stark was naturally anxious that both his clients should make the film, and to ease the conflict he invented all sorts of muddled billing clauses in the hope that both Mason and Douglas would each think he had come out on top. In the end, Kirk's ego proved to be bigger than Mason's. Mason became fascinated with his complex part, and Douglas won the battle for top billing when Mason decided that the role was worth more than the size of his name. Besides, when it came down to it, Walt Disney really had bigger billing than any of the actors.

Kirk's fee for doing the film was 175,000 dollars, and he had a ball making the picture. He and Peter Lorre were the only members of the cast to enjoy a couple of weeks of location shooting in Jamaica while Mason and Lucas had to be content with the confines of the Disney studio. Kirk also had fun visiting Walt's home where Disney owned a marvellous miniature railway which was large enough to sit on and ride. It was Disney's favourite toy, and he invited Kirk to take a ride, which Kirk gladly did. While Kirk rode up and down on the miniature track, Disney took some home movie film of the event, and they both had a wonderful time.

Despite the impressive cast, the real star of the picture was the giant squid which attempts to drag Mason into the depths of the sea while Douglas stabs at it with his harpoon. A huge water tank had been specially designed at Disney's studio for this sequence, and Disney's special effects department had created a giant mechanical squid. Both Mason and Douglas received a severe soaking as director Richard Fleischer turned his cameras on the scene. But when Disney viewed the rushes he was distinctly unimpressed with the results. He felt the squid looked too much like a dummy, and he ordered his art director John Meeham and effects genius Ub Iwerks to rebuild the monster. This they did at enormous cost, and Kirk and James had to undergo yet another soaking in the studio tank. But the results were well worth the effort and added expense.

The film managed to preserve the feeling of Jules Verne's original story, which he wrote in 1870. Unlike other pictures based on books by Jules Verne, or even H. G. Wells, there was no superficial arbitrary romance concocted for any of the main characters. Kirk Douglas had to be content with kissing a seal rather than a girl.

Douglas also had the opportunity to use his singing voice, which had not been particularly evident in his acting career since his stage debut playing a singing messengerboy. In this Disney classic he strums a whalebone guitar and belts out a lively sea shanty, 'A Whale Of A Tale'.

It was also an opportunity for him to be thoroughly likeable for once, though there was a typical roguishness about him. He is also very much the hero of the piece, contrasting starkly with James Mason who produces yet another masterly villainous portrayal. Here, though, Mason is never actually bad at heart: his intentions, to rid the world of war, are honourable, but his methods despicable. Mason succeeds in gaining a certain amount of sympathy, and it was this aspect which finally converted him to playing the part, giving Kirk the top billing he was demanding.

The film also sparked off an initial reaction from Kirk regarding his director, Richard Fleischer. Fleischer's previous work had been in the main crime and suspense dramas. *20,000 Leagues Under The Sea* was his first attempt at a colourful adventure picture. Kirk was so impressed with Fleischer that he would, in the next few years, hire him to direct Kirk's own production of *The Vikings*.

It is unfortunate that after the completion of this pre-*Star Wars* fantasy epic, Kirk and Disney had a falling out. Disney's home movie footage of Kirk on the miniature train turned up on one of Walt's television shows without Disney getting Kirk's permission or paying him a fee for his surprise appearance. Perhaps a good many other Hollywood actors might not have taken umbrage at this, but Kirk was very much a businessman. He'd gained nothing from his appearance in the TV show, and he sued Disney for using the footage. Disney was then, and remained so, one of Hollywood's most popular figures and certainly never set out to stab anyone in the back. He was certainly not used to being sued, unlike most other movie moguls, and Kirk's action did little to endear himself to any of Disney's friends in the business.

But the important thing in all this was that the picture was a monster hit, unlike *The Racers* which Kirk did at 20th Century-Fox. This was the clichéd story of an affair between a Grand Prix racer, played by Douglas, and a ballerina, played by Bella Darvi. At the time, Miss Darvi was not the happiest of leading ladies for Kirk to find himself opposite. She was about to be thrown out by Fox after just two previous films for them. She had been discovered by Fox mogul Darryl F. Zanuck and her name had been derived from the names of Darryl and Virginia Zanuck. But there was definite discord between Darvi and Zanuck's wife, with rumours flying thick and fast of an affair between Darvi and her boss. Kirk just grinned and bore it.

At least *Man Without A Star* had him back in the saddle where he now felt quite at home. It also gave him the opportunity to warble a little, as he had done previously in *20,000 Leagues Under The Sea*. This time, though, he had to play the banjo as well, and so he learned to play, adding yet another skill which would prove generally useless since he'd not get much of an opportunity to practise it once the film was over. Kirk Douglas has never been much in demand for his singing! He also spent a great deal of time learning to leap on to a horse like the Lone Ranger, and to twirl his guns in a most elaborate fashion.

Man Without A Star turned out to be a superior western thanks to director King Vidor who managed to create some of the sweaty, sexual overtones which had made his *Duel In The Sun* such an enormous success. Kirk played a drifter who allows himself to be seduced by rancher Jeanne Crain into working for her. However, he changes sides when he leads the local homesteaders against her after she expands her herd so much that it spills over into the homesteaders' lands. Also in the film was Claire Trevor, then pushing forty-six but still portraying the kind of bad girl with the good heart she immortalized in John Ford's *Stagecoach* sixteen years earlier.

Kirk thoroughly enjoyed making this outdoors actioner, and as was his custom by now, he sat up much of the night studying the script and attempting to rewrite lines and situations. The next day he'd present them to King Vidor who was the kind of director who had everything planned out in his own mind and was unwilling to change anything which he felt was already just how he wanted it.

'I felt throughout the filming of *Man Without A Star* that Kirk was working himself up to being a director,' says Vidor. 'This sometimes causes minor conflicts since the director has probably planned the scene weeks before and is not usually in the mood to make last-minute changes.'

Although Vidor rejected Kirk's ideas, the veteran director does praise Douglas as 'a tireless worker and a first-rate performer. Kirk comes across with aggressive strength,' he adds. 'It is rather difficult, I imagine, to project an aggressive image in scene after scene all day from nine to six and not have some of it rub off on yourself.'

Aggressive he certainly is, but back in 1955 when he made *Man Without A Star* he was just as aggressive with himself as he was with those he worked with. He was climbing a higher hill to become the actor he had long dreamed of being—a truly independent actor. That same year he achieved his goal when Bryna, named after his mother, made its first film, *The Indian Fighter*. Kirk Douglas, the independent actor and the fledgling film producer had arrived. When I once asked him why it was so important for him to produce his own pictures, he told me:

> The reason for having a production company is to participate more in the selection and development of material and to be engaged more in the creative process.
> I guess people think that it's a financial thing and you become a big movie mogul. Well I never became a big mogul with my little company, but it is an entity through which I can produce movies.

Certainly *The Indian Fighter* was the kind of picture which Kirk enjoyed making, and now that he was in charge he was able to indulge himself by getting involved in every aspect of the production. The only thing it didn't have was a particularly challenging role for Kirk to play, but then with this his first production, he didn't need the added responsibility of giving any kind of in-depth performance. This was just to be a great piece of commercial cinema. He was in a way playing safe for once in his choice of movie, and he was certainly playing safe in his choice of director, Andre de Toth, who had done his best work in gutsy westerns.

Kirk was featured in the film as a mercenary, confident roguish scout whose rough exterior belies his integrity. When the Sioux refuse to allow a wagon train to pass through their territory, the army calls for Douglas to liase with the Indians. Douglas succeeds in getting the chief to agree to peace, but as in all good cowboy and Injun films, there are bad guys on both sides. Walter Matthau plays an unscrupulous white man who is partly responsible for causing trouble with the Sioux, although there is also the chief's pugnacious warrior brother who doesn't want peace at any price.

In viewing this film, it seems unbelievable that Kirk as a small boy in Amsterdam should have been such a skinny, puny kid. His physical progression over the years was clearly displayed in *The Indian Fighter* in more ways than one.

In a confrontation with Harry Landers as the rebellious brother to the Indian chief, Kirk put his ability as a wrestler to perfect use, although he had to learn to wrestle Indian fashion. True to form, Kirk delved deep into Indian life to research for the film, and the ability he acquired to Indian wrestle demonstrated not just his dedication to the job at hand but also his fitness.

His physique was also on display in what was then—1955—considered to be a sizzling scene. Kirk and an Indian maid, with whom he has fallen in love, frolic naked in a river. To play Onahti, the chief's daughter whom Douglas spies bathing in the river and later engages in some then titillating but now tame water sports, Kirk hired Italian beauty Elsa Martinelli. She was then twenty-three and had had no previous acting experience. She was working as a model when Kirk's wife, Anne, saw her and was impressed with her sultry Italian looks which could pass for being Red Indian. Her nude scenes were shot under tight security to guard against peeping Toms who may have found themselves in Oregon when the film was being shot. It was the first time Kirk had ever appeared in the buff, although he was coyly photographed. He was then aged thirty-nine and in great physical shape. Amazingly, more than twenty years later he would appear completely nude in *Saturn 3*.

With this, his first production, Kirk was more interested in entertainment than art. His future as a producer certainly depended a great deal on this picture, and as he has said, 'If a movie doesn't make money, you have failed. It's a fact that the lack of revenue means not enough people have seen that picture, and that's what you make them for, to be seen.'

That Kirk should choose a western for his first attempt at producing is not surprising. Westerns were, in the Fifties, big business. Kirk has his own theory as to why westerns should prove so successful world-wide. He told me:

> I think a western is popular world-wide because it's a very interesting part of American history. You see, life has become so complicated. What we love about the western is that it was an age of action when, if you had a problem, you

didn't say, 'I'm gonna see my lawyer and take out a deposition.' Men dealt with it directly. They faced each other. And there's something about that directness that appeals to people.

Filmed in Oregon, *The Indian Fighter* became something of a family affair. First Kirk took on Anne as the casting director. And for the key role of a widow who falls for the rugged, taciturn Indian scout, Douglas hired his former wife, Diana. It was Anne who suggested that Kirk cast Diana in the movie. To those who knew the Douglases, this was no great surprise. Diana and Kirk were good friends and the two women got on well together. There had been no personal bitterness between Kirk and his first wife following the divorce, and Kirk had remained a proud and worthy father to Michael and Joel who now lived in Connecticut with their mother. However, during summer holidays the boys came to stay with their dad. Kirk was usually working and so the boys always went on location with him or just hung around the studio where Kirk was working.

So congenial was the relationship between the Douglases and Diana that when Kirk and Anne once went to France, Diana and 'the boys came and stayed in Kirk's Hollywood bungalow. The Douglases were just as friendly with Anne's former husband, Albert Buydens, and whenever they were in Europe they made a point of visiting Albert in Belgium.

As casting director on *The Indian Fighter*, Anne felt the role of the widow was tailor-made for Diana and talked it over with Kirk. He agreed and offered her the role, but not until he'd tested her first. There was a snag. The boys were still at school and Diana would have to travel with the production company up to Oregon. Anne, who was pregnant, came up with the solution. She wasn't fit to travel so she offered to look after the boys while Diana was making the film on location. When the holidays did come around the boys got to go to Oregon to be with their dad. It was experiences like these that prepared both of Kirk's sons to go into the business themselves, much against their father's will.

'There were always paparazzi around dad,' recalls Michael. 'When you talk about the advantages of being second generation, coping with fame—that's a big one. Watching how my father handled himself, I'm sure I inherited by osmosis his understanding of what is professional behaviour.'

Diana Douglas never did make much of an impact in movies, but she remained good friends with her ex-husband. Although Anne was now his wife, he never forgot that Diana was the mother of Michael and Joel. As far as Kirk is concerned, the family would be incomplete without Diana.

'Why shouldn't we all be on good terms?' asks Anne when someone displays surprise at the remarkable relationship they share:

> Kirk was divorced long before he met me and my marriage was on the rocks before Kirk entered my life. Both our divorces were congenial affairs. And we all like one another.
>
> It's rather typical of Kirk that he would hire Diana in his first production. He has a sense of loyalty and responsibility to his family that borders on a guilt complex. You don't have to be a psychiatrist to realize this is a compensation for his own father's lack of loyalty and responsibility.
>
> Kirk is first and foremost a family man.

It's his love for his sons that has spurred him to do his best to discourage his children from being actors. When Michael, at the age of twelve, played his first role in Shakespeare's *As You Like It*, Kirk was dismayed to see how much his son was enjoying the experience. After the performance Michael, who could always expect nothing but praise from dad, was astounded when Kirk told him, 'You were terrible.' Of course, Kirk didn't mean that. As he says, 'I was very pleased because I thought that would bring him to his senses, and he'd just go off and be a good lawyer!' The Douglas family grew in the year 1955 when Anne gave birth to Peter on 23 November.

Kirk was delighted with the way *The Indian Fighter* turned out. Unusually for a 1950s western, it expressed both interest and sympathy for the Indian at a time when the only good Injuns in films were dead ones. Undoubtedly, the persecution of the Indians was something which Kirk could, by his inheritance, identify with. But he nevertheless made it a commercial film with plenty of thundering action and those daring scenes which helped to bring sex into Westerns and so lift this opus into an adult category.

Bryna's next production wouldn't be for another couple of years, and since it was to be a lavishly mounted historical saga about the Vikings and would cost a considerable amount of money and require very careful pre-production planning, there was time to make films for other people. And in the process he ended up with what is probably his finest ever performance, as artist Van Gogh, plus the cinema's greatest anti-war film and a western that would become a classic.

When MGM announced its plans to make *Lust For Life*, a biography of Vincent Van Gogh, Kirk was first in the queue for the part. It was a part he just *had* to play. He told me, 'Van Gogh is such a fascinating character. So much is known about him. While the script was being developed I took a look at a picture of Van Gogh. I grew a beard, cut my hair and dyed it red, and I looked like Van Gogh. And I guess the film makers thought so too.'

They certainly did. As the film's director, Vincente Minnelli, recalls, 'Once we got the green light to proceed with the picture, there was no question if Kirk would play Van Gogh. No other actor was even considered for the part.'

Kirk went to extraordinary lengths to prepare for his role. He was given access to five volumes of letters which Van Gogh had written to his brother Theo, often writing in contradictory terms about his views on life and painting, stating with great conviction one point of view and then literally arguing with himself by stating just the opposite. If these letters didn't exactly help to clarify Van Gogh's seemingly schizophrenic personality, they certainly confirmed his two-toned nature, giving Douglas the colours he needed to paint his own movie portrait.

He also wanted to be seen painting the pictures, and so he had a French artist teach him to paint crows just as Van Gogh would have painted them. He ended up painting more than eight hundred crows before he got it right, and then proudly exclaimed, 'I am not one of the art's great immortals, but at least I can catch a crow in flight!' The scene in which Van Gogh paints the crows is the tortured climax when Van Gogh has a fit of madness, believing the crows to be harbingers of death. It was his last painting. Shortly after he committed suicide. It was the very first scene to be shot, filmed in Arles in Southern France where a wheatfield had been chemically preserved out of season for Kirk to stand in and paint his crows.

With his own firm views of Van Gogh's character, Kirk was forever putting forward his own ideas as to how certain scenes should be shot or what could be added here and there. Minnelli was a director who knew and liked Kirk and readily accepted those ideas which he felt were valid. In fact, Douglas and Minnelli agreed on many aspects of the picture in its telling. *Lust For Life* is a film in which there are many touches which were Kirk's own ideas and which were accepted without his having to fight for them.

It was a perfect actor-director relationship because Minnelli had been hard at work on a previous film and was unable to make full preparation to make this picture in cooperation with the producer and Norman Corwin, the author of the screenplay. It was virtually only after he landed in Arles to begin filming the story of Van Gogh that Minnelli began seeking the subtle nuances that would bring the film to life. In this Kirk Douglas became his ally. Kirk and Minnelli spent many hours together studying Van Gogh's paintings and drawing in books, and they often visited museums where originals of Van Gogh's work hung, allowing Douglas and Minnelli to try and analyze the way in which the artist used every nerve in his body and his ferocious energy to paint his immortal pictures.

In between takes, John Houseman, Vincente Minnelli and Kirk Douglas, the last dressed in dowdy clothes with his dimple hidden behind a fuzz of red beard, would gather to work on the next scenes. Houseman also happened to be a good writer and was able to rework the scenes and dialogue as necessary, and it was during these sessions that Douglas and Minnelli made their contributions.

As hard as it may be for many other film directors to believe, Vincente Minnelli claimed that working with Kirk Douglas was his most rewarding and stimulating collaboration. Minnelli is also ecstatic in his praise for Kirk. 'He is blessed with tireless energy, a willingness to try anything and a complete disregard for his own looks,' he says. 'He couldn't care less about being the handsome hero. His enthusiasm and devotion to the project is contagious and transmits itself to the crew, the cast, and everyone connected with the picture.'

Not everyone was as delighted about Kirk's portrayal of Van Gogh. John Wayne, the cinema's greatest man's man, saw the picture at a special preview at which Kirk was present. Wayne was astounded at what he saw up on the screen, watching Kirk doing unmanly things like cutting off his ear and later killing himself. He was genuinely appalled at this pathetic character which tough guy Kirk Douglas was portraying. After the screening Wayne motioned Kirk to join him on the terrace. When they were out of earshot, Wayne growled, 'Kirk, how in the hell could you play such a weak character like that?'

Kirk staggered back in amazement. 'What do you mean, John?'

'Fellers like us,' said Wayne, 'are the tough guys of movies. We're in a certain class.'

'But John,' said Kirk, 'I'm an actor. I try to play all different kinds of parts.'

Remembering that incident, Kirk told me, 'Wayne has very prescribed concepts as to what he should play, whereas I feel an actor should play anything.

'He didn't like it when I played Van Gogh in *Lust For Life* because he would have preferred me to be more like one of the boys, so to speak.'

Today Kirk remains unmoveably proud of his performance of Van Gogh:

> As I look back, I think, 'Who else could have played him?' There are certain roles that make you feel 'that's *my* part'. I'm not saying the assessment is correct, but that's the emotional feeling you get. As an actor it's one of my favourite parts. I only saw the film once because it's too painful for me to watch. It meant a lot to me, and it represented all the suffering that all artists go through in an attempt to express themselves, and to get some kind of recognition. Van Gogh had all those troubles.

Again the American Academy of Motion Picture Arts and Sciences nominated Kirk for an Oscar. Again the Best Actor award went elsewhere. But he could find some solace with an award for Best Actor from the New York Critics and some of the best notices he had ever received.

His friend Minnelli expressed his feelings thus: 'In my opinion, Kirk should have won the Academy Award. He was the only possible choice to play Van Gogh because of his physical appearance and then for his great violence because Van Gogh, like Douglas, was very fierce in his loves and hates. A wonderful performance.'

Unfortunately, despite all the raves from the press, *Lust For Life* did not gell with the movie-going public of 1956. However, the film, and Kirk's performance, have gone down in the annals of movie history as classics, but it was not enough to continue paying the bills. Kirk needed another big hit.

And he found it. Ironically, it came in the form of an offer from the man whom Kirk broke his first movie contract with, Hal B. Wallis. What's more, it was an offer which Kirk initially turned down.

Explained Kirk, 'Hal was trying to set up *Gunfight At The OK Corral*. They sent the script to me and I turned it down. Then they sent it to Burt Lancaster and he turned it down.

'Then I reread the script and I thought, "Wait a minute. If Burt and I played in it I think we could make this a fun picture."

'So I said to Burt, "If you play the part of Wyatt Earp then I'll play the part of Doc Holliday," and he said, "Okay."

'So we made *Gunfight At The OK Corral*.'

Lancaster also had an ulterior motive in making the picture. He desperately wanted to play the part of Starbuck, the lead in *The Rainmaker* which Hal Wallis had bought from Broadway. After hearing from Kirk, Lancaster rang Hal Wallis in the dead of night and announced that if Wallis would give him the role of Starbuck, he'd do *Gunfight At The OK Corral*. Wallis agreed.

The legend of Wyatt Earp's and Doc Holliday's shoot-out at the OK Corral had been recreated by film makers before, particularly by John Ford in his classic *My Darling Clementine*. Ford always claimed that he based his filmed gunfight on an account given to him first-hand by an aged Wyatt Earp when

Ford was just a kid. But Hal Wallis thought he could make a more realistic picture about the same episode. At least that was the plan when Leon Uris wrote the script and John Sturges was hired to direct the film.

Kirk Douglas and Burt Lancaster had other ideas. As I said, Kirk thought that he and Lancaster could make this a fun western. They came into the production exactly as Sheilah Graham had described them. They were the terrible-tempered twins, and they exerted their authority throughout filming. Kirk was now an established creative film producer and Burt had directed himself in *The Kentuckian* as well as producing a number of his own pictures. They were also two of the biggest movie stars around. John Sturges was in for a rough ride. Determined to wring every moment of fun out of the script, Kirk and Burt sat up most nights rewriting their dialogue. Most mornings began with a fight between the Douglas-Lancaster team against the Wallis-Sturges team. According to Wallis, Sturges ensured that no word of the original script was changed, but there is no doubt that the finished picture was hardly an exercise in authenticity. It was, however, the fun picture which Kirk had first envisioned.

In transferring the historical events that occurred in Tombstone during the late nineteenth century to the screen, Kirk Douglas for once discarded his usual immersion into research, since authenticity was just about the last thing he was aiming for. He played Wyatt Earp in the traditional manner, portraying the true-life lawman as upright, loyal and honest beyond reproach. In truth, Earp had been corrupt, mercenary and unscrupulous, very much like the lawman Kirk would play eighteen years later in *Posse*. Earp was also known to be the owner of a brothel. The thing was, in 1957 audiences would not have accepted such characters as worthy protagonists for a movie, unlike today where the anti-hero has become a part of film tradition.

Doc Holliday, as portrayed by Lancaster, has also been romanticized and is seen as something of an idealist and an aristocrat; the real Doc Holliday is believed to have been a mean, murderous character who failed at dentistry.

The highlight of the film was of course the actual gunfight at the OK Corral. It remains one of the cinema's most exciting western shoot-outs and took weeks of preparation and actual filming time, lasting some quarter of an hour on the screen. Again, this was poetic licence: the actual gunfight was all but over in a matter of minutes.

It becomes clear when watching the film that Kirk was enjoying himself immensely. He particularly enjoyed working again with Burt. Before this film they had been able to maintain the friendship they had struck when they made *I Walk Alone* ten years earlier. But on the set of *Gunfight* they were able to strengthen the bond between them. In making the film they found themselves in Arizona where all the location shooting was done. There they and the rest of the cast and crew were put up in a hotel. Kirk and Burt found that they shared adjoining rooms. While most of the other members of the film unit were bedded down at nights, Kirk and Burt sat up until the early hours of the morning discussing their families, their work, their hopes and their dreams. It was out there in Arizona that their friendship really ripened.

Kirk told me, 'I've enjoyed working with Burt. He's fun. He's aggressive. Sparks fly. I like that. It's fun, exciting. We always had fun. *Loud* fun. We were together a lot after the day's shooting. We'd have dinner and we'd talk until three or four in the morning.'

Kirk has described his relationship with Burt as 'love-hate'. There were times when Kirk was deeply hurt by certain witticisms made by his pal. Such a time was when the two stars had just finished shooting a scene from *Gunfight At The OK Corral*, and as they walked off the set they were pursued by a crowd of fans begging for autographs. Burt's problem was that he didn't easily respond to strangers, especially autograph hunters. He turned to those pressing in around him and said, 'Go and ask Mr Douglas for his autograph. He's a great actor. Of course, you probably didn't recognize him without his built-up shoes.' Kirk, who is much shorter than Lancaster, was visibly upset by the remark. But it wasn't enough to cause a feud between the terrible-tempered twins.

The picture proved to be a smash hit at the box office. It was exactly what Kirk needed, and it also enhanced John Sturges's reputation. Despite the arguments he had with both his stars, he would in the years ahead work with them again, only he was very careful to ensure that he didn't work with them both at the same time.

Kirk's next picture, *Top Secret Affair*, was hardly a star vehicle for him. It was originally intended to star Humphrey Bogart and Lauren Bacall. Warner Bros had bought the rights to a witty novel, *Melville Goodwin, USA*, which became *Top Secret Affair*, for the fabulous Bogarts. But when Bogey fell ill with what would prove to be terminal cancer, Kirk and Susan Hayward were assigned by Warners to make the movie. Sadly, and ironically, the film was released in January 1957: that's when Bogey died.

Mind you, Bogart could probably have done without the movie, which did little more than give audiences another rare glimpse of Douglas's comedy talents. In this picture he played, typically, a tough, virile Major General who wins a government appointment, much to the chagrin of magazine publisher Susan Hayward, who sets about attempting to discredit the Major General. Using her journalistic instincts, she lures him to her plush home, determined to discover from him anything she could use as ammunition. But, inevitably, she falls for him and only continues with her campaign when he walks out on her.

The film quite successfully poked fun at the publishing world, at Congress and at the military. Kirk has certainly played his fair share of military types, but probably never more powerfully than he did in his next film, *Paths Of Glory*, made in 1957. Like so many of Kirk's most potent films, such as *Ace In The Hole* and *Lust For Life*, *Paths Of Glory* began as a flop on its initial release, yet has emerged as one of the cinema's great masterpieces.

Film director Stanley Kubrick, an unknown 29-year-old movie enthusiast whose previous work was generally low budget and high art, was desperate to make *Paths Of Glory*, based on a book which told of a harrowing incident involving French troops in the trenches of the First World War. Kubrick knew that through this film he could make one of the first authentic anti-war pictures in which some of the good guys were also the bad guys. Unlike other war pictures, this one would have its big battle sequence early on in the film and have as its climax the execution of a handful of French soldiers found guilty of desertion. The deserters would be the good guys and the officers would be the heavies. It was a unique story.

It scared the daylights out of every studio Kubrick took it to. But then Kirk Douglas got to hear about it and he read the script. To Kubrick's delight, Douglas announced he wanted to play the role of Colonel Dax, the French officer who observes every futile moment of the film, from the spectacular, frightening battle, through the mock justice of the court-martials, to the final degrading sacrifices of the condemned soldiers.

For Kubrick and Kirk, it was the beginning of a short, profitable and ultimately bitter relationship. Today Kubrick, for reasons which shall become apparent later on, finds it hard to speak kindly of the man who really got him started in what's proved to be a gloriously successful career. Kirk, however, is full of praise for Kubrick's abilities but, when speaking about his association with the young director, makes clear his position. Talking to me about his work with Kubrick, Kirk said:

> I'm the one who set up Kubrick's *Paths Of Glory* because he couldn't get the money. I went to United Artists and raised the financing. Yet before we'd started shooting he'd rewritten the whole script, and I refused to do it.
>
> He said, 'I want to make it a commercial movie.' So I said, 'Look, I don't know if it's commercial or not. The first script was beautiful and that's the one we're gonna use.'
>
> So we did. And in my humble opinion *Paths Of Glory* is the best directed film he's ever done.

Paths Of Glory cost a mere 900,000 dollars. A third of that went to Kirk as his fee. Kubrick received no salary but did get a share of the profits, which initially were few. However, it did start Kubrick off and running although it was Kirk who later stepped in a second time to save Kubrick's career.

For the remarkable battle scene in which the French make a futile attack on Ant Hill, a large stretch of ground was rented near the German village of Pucheim. All vegetation was destroyed and any standing barns were demolished. Trees were shattered with explosives, and sixty workmen spent three weeks digging up the ground into a swamp, hewing out trenches and littering the place with barbed wire. German policemen were hired to play the troops and six cameras were set up, including one tracking camera, to shoot the terrible and bloody battle of Ant Hill. Five 'dying zones' were mapped out and each extra who had to die was given a piece of paper which informed him in which zone he would fall.

So incensed were the French authorities over the way in which officers in the French army had been portrayed in the film that it was banned in France for almost twenty years. When it finally opened in the late Seventies, French audiences flocked to see it. Curiously, American and British audiences weren't quite so enthusiastic when the film was first released in 1957. But like so many other films starring Kirk Douglas, it gained cult status and is now considered by many to be the best film ever to come out of America.

But a recognition did not come immediately to Kubrick. He didn't get another directing job until Kirk hired him almost three years later, while Douglas continued to work solidly and successfully, mostly for himself.

SEVEN/Bryna

With his 'little company', Bryna, Kirk Douglas began moving into the really big league. He had for some time been preparing to film *The Vikings*, and in 1958 with the assistance of experienced producer Jerry Bresler, Kirk set his classic 'Norse Opera' in motion.

Looking for a director he felt secure with for this spectacular yarn which would cost in the region of four million dollars, he looked to Richard Fleischer with whom he'd enjoyed a satisfying professional relationship making *20,000 Leagues Under The Sea*. But even with experts like Bresler and Fleischer at the helm, Kirk was the boss. And since he had so much at stake, he was entitled to give the orders. He had put up some of his own money alongside that of United Artists. It was his biggest gamble to date. He was laying his whole career on the line, and he involved himself in every aspect of production.

Impressed with Charlton Heston's obvious qualities as an 'epic' actor as displayed in *The Ten Commandments*, Kirk offered him the role of Eric, a Viking slave who turns out to be a British king and half-brother to Einar, played by Douglas himself. But after Heston turned down the role Kirk offered it to Tony Curtis, who came highly recommended by Kirk's pal Burt Lancaster, who himself had gambled twice on Curtis in his own production, *Trapeze* and *The Sweet Smell Of Success*, and won both times. The role of Morgana, a Welsh princess who rejects Einar and falls for Eric, was easy to fill. Curtis's wife Janet Leigh had co-starred on numerous occasions with her husband, and so Douglas cast her in the leading lady's role.

Virtually every part was filled by someone Kirk could consider a safe bet. Rugged and rotund Ernest Borgnine was the barbaric Viking chief; stiff-upper-lip actor James Donald was Lord Egbert; and in the role of the fiendish British king Aella was Australian actor Frank Thring. This part led to Thring landing all the best villainous parts in many of the historical and biblical epics of the late Fifties and early Sixties.

Douglas, a stickler for authenticity, ensured that no Viking warrior featured in his film wore any horned helmets, since historians had already proved that these worshippers of Odin never did in fact wear such horned helms. Authentic Viking ships also had to be constructed, and so replicas of real Viking ships on display in Oslo's Viking Museum were built, measuring some seventy-five feet in length. These long ships had one modification; they had motorized engines hidden in their bows. Determined to have his Vikings look like real Norsemen, Douglas engaged two hundred members of rowing clubs in Norway and Denmark who could easily handle the sleek sea-going vessels.

To describe the film as a 'Norse Opera' is certainly not derogatory, since Kirk himself says, '*The Vikings* I enjoyed because it's a sort of Scandinavian western. I always think of that time as being similar to our wild west period.'

Kirk wanted everything to be just right, and he took the entire cast and crew off to Norway where cinematographer Jack Cardiff captured some exquisite shots of long ships sailing up the fjords. However, not everything ran according to schedule. Douglas had planned to spend one month in Norway for the vital sequences of Viking life in a settlement along the fjords: instead, they stayed for two months. Kirk's greatest enemy was the weather. For days they waited for the sun to shine, and when it did everyone jumped to their positions. The wind was also a problem. It blew strong and constantly down those fjords. As the long ships were motorized, the rowers had quite an easy time of it, but as Jack Cardiff once said to me, 'It was the funniest thing to see a ship going forward with the sail billowing the wrong way.'

That extra month in Norway boosted the budget by one

million dollars, and Kirk had to take desperate measures to find the extra money. He went into hock, pledging every asset he had, both present and future, including anything he might make by hiring himself out to other producers. It was a frustrating time for Kirk. 'In sixty days we only got eleven days of sunshine,' he recalls. 'Two of them were on Sunday when we couldn't shoot.'

Eventually they left the rainy fjords of Norway behind and headed for the coast of Brittany where scenes of the English castle being besieged were to be staged. No suitable castle could be found in Britain, and so Forte La Lotte was chosen for its spectacular design and its amazing preservation. Unfortunately, when they got to Brittany they found the weather just as bad, if not worse. Again the entire unit stood in the rain for days waiting for a break in the weather. Kirk added up the cost of the delays. It was costing him 45,000 dollars a day.

But despite the gloom, he maintained a cheerful countenance. Surveying his rain-soaked unit, he remarked, 'We've got a small army up here and a fleet of ships. We could probably attack one of the smaller countries with some success.'

Tony Curtis had nothing but admiration and praise for Kirk, whom he now considered a firm friend. 'A couple of years ago they'd have called Kirk the greatest organizing genius of his time,' he was heard to say. 'They'd have said he was a Napoleon.'

Kirk also found time to send himself up for the benefit of the visiting newspapermen. He told them, 'Now I'm producing my own pictures I can rarely afford to hire myself. Apart from that, as a producer I can't stand myself as an actor. I'm too temperamental.'

One day, sitting on a soaked bench while the rain washed away his money at five thousand dollars an hour, he said, 'I started at the bottom. I had nowhere else to go but up. If I lose everything, so what?' When at last the rain finally cleared, Richard Fleischer moved his cameras in for the climactic battle. Kirk insisted on performing his own stunts when he and Curtis fight it out atop a tower a couple of hundred feet off the ground. Curtis himself was no coward when it came to staging film fights. He was quite an expert with the sword and helped to guide Kirk through the dangerous sequence. Both men showed remarkable courage in completing an entire screen sword fight without the use of doubles, and at considerable risk to their lives.

The future of Bryna now depended on the success of *The Vikings*, so while Kirk waited for the film to be edited and released, he went back to work for Hal B. Wallis to earn some money to pay off some of his debts caused by the escalating costs of *The Vikings*. Wallis wanted quite naturally to repeat the success he had had with *Gunfight At The OK Corral*, and so he put into production *Last Train From Gun Hill*, with Kirk again being directed by John Sturges. Charles Lang, Jr, who had photographed *Gunfight*, was also cinematographer on this western. However, Burt Lancaster was unavailable to co-star this time, so Wallis chose Anthony Quinn to play the second male lead. Quinn had worked with Kirk twice before, on *Ulysses* and *Lust For Life*. With his Mexican-Irish-American lineage, he was a lusty, fiery personality who wouldn't shy away from a fight. He had a healthy respect for Kirk, who reciprocated. Kirk didn't enjoy with Quinn the same kind of close relationship he had with Burt, but in Quinn he found a friend with an appealing professional aggressiveness.

The film itself was quite different from *Gunfight At The OK Corral*. With this film Wallis and Sturges succeeded in capturing the dramatic and suspenseful atmosphere they had originally envisioned for *Gunfight*. Undoubtedly Kirk was more agreeable in adhering to the original concept of *Last Train From Gunhill* because this was in essence a tragic story and not one of mirth.

Douglas played another Marshal, but one who is widowed very early in the picture when his Indian wife is raped and murdered by two young roughnecks. Douglas traces their steps to Gunhill, where he discovers one of the culprits to be the son of his old friend, played by Quinn. Their friendship rapidly grows sour as Douglas vows to find his wife's killers and bring them to justice.

Last Train From Gun Hill actually proved to be a superior film to *Gunfight At The OK Corral*. Kirk gave a different type of performance from those of his previous westerns. He skilfully displays a restrained tension, like a man haunted and living in limbo. Even when he is forced to gun down the killers and catches the last train from Gun Hill, he leaves the picture on a sombre, downbeat note.

The picture proved to be a box office success, but even more important, *The Vikings* was now doing fantastic business, to Kirk's great relief. It encouraged him to start work on another production in 1959, *The Devil's Disciple*, from the play by George Bernard Shaw. It was something of a surprising choice for Kirk to pick as a further vehicle for Bryna. For a start, *The Devil's Disciple* was not even a play which Shaw himself liked. Also, Kirk had previously played safe with his own productions by making outdoor adventure yarns. Kirk couldn't resist a gamble, but this was one which didn't come off. He could only console himself with the fact that he was a joint loser with Hecht-Hill-Lancaster Films, with whom he co-produced the film.

Burt Lancaster had been trying to get *The Devil's Disciple* into production for some time, having paid 600,000 dollars to Shaw's estate for the property. He had wanted the play to be rewritten quite drastically, but was unable to find anyone capable of performing such a feat. So he shelved it until Kirk came along and said that he was interested in playing the role of Dick Dudgeon if Burt would play the part of the minister. Initially Burt was going to play Dudgeon and Montgomery Clift was to have played the minister, but Clift was having severe mental problems, so Burt took up the offer. Kirk was instrumental in getting the necessary backing for the film, although they ended up working on such a limited budget that neither star made much money out of it. The only actor who was paid a decent fee for his services was Laurence Olivier, who had the role of the general.

The Devil's Disciple was not made without considerable difficulties. It was filmed in England with a shooting schedule strictly limited to forty-eight days. The director, Alexander MacKendrick, who had previously directed Burt Lancaster in the stylish *Sweet Smell Of Success*, was shooting brilliant stuff, but after one week he had accomplished the equivalent of only two days' work. He was promptly fired by Lancaster and Douglas, and the British press made a meal of the story, branding the two stars and Lancaster's partners as dastardly and unprofessional. The fact was that MacKendrick had agreed to shoot to schedule and had failed to do so, although Lancaster later admitted that MacKendrick's few scenes were the best in the entire picture, which was handed over to Guy Hamilton.

There were problems too with Olivier which had nothing to do with temperament. Olivier was, and remains, a total professional, but he was at that time undergoing a great deal of mental and emotional turmoil over the breakdown of his marriage to Vivien Leigh. He was experiencing extreme difficulty in keeping his mind on his work. He kept confusing Kirk with Burt and vice versa. This irritated Lancaster no end, and every time Olivier called him Kirk, he'd glare back and in that clipped tone of his say, '*Burt!*'

While *The Devil's Disciple* was in production *The Vikings* was treated to a royal premiere in London and subsequently enjoyed the same kind of success it was meeting with back in the States. With *The Vikings* now an undisputed hit, Kirk was able to let his mask slip a little. 'I'm not as brave as I am in some of my own pictures,' he confessed. 'If *The Vikings* had been a flop, I would have lost an even million dollars of my own, and it would have broken my spirit.'

Elated by the success of not just the film, but of himself, he remarked, 'Man, Prince Philip came to the premiere of *The Vikings* and here I am in my own Bentley. It all seems so damned unreal. Like it's all a mistake. Like some little man is going to tap me on the shoulder and say, "Okay boy, it's all over. Get back where you belong."'

It was one of the very few times when Kirk Douglas would reveal his true feelings; he would, for the most part, continue to maintain his tough image. He even went as far, during the Sixties, as to positively insist that he was mean, tough, unpopular and thoroughly unlikeable. Kirk Douglas became an expert at selling his image.

But the image that only close friends ever saw was the devoted father. Life with Anne was satisfying and fulfilling, and, most important for a Hollywood marriage, enduring. It was sustained all the more when on 21 June 1958, Eric was born.

Kirk now started looking in other areas of motion picture entertainment. He had an ambition to put all his resources into making a picture that would prove even bigger than *The Vikings*.

To this end he had bought the rights to a book which at one time had been all but banned as Communist propaganda. That book was *Spartacus*.

But before embarking on the most ambitious project of his entire career, he put Bryna to work alongside of Quine Productions to make the provocative though now dated sexual drama, *Strangers When We Meet*, produced and directed by Richard Quine. Kirk recognized the commercial potential of this screen version of Evan Hunter's novel because it displayed a daring frankness in dealing with adultery. But it was not originally intended as a Kirk Douglas picture. Glenn Ford was originally signed to play the role of an architect who cheats on his wife by having a fling with the beautiful blonde next door. The blonde was to be played by Kim Novak, of whom Quine was reputedly enamoured. Ford refused point blank to work with Novak, who as the Sixties drew nigh was on a rapid decline. She also had a reputation for being difficult. And since Richard Quine had no intention of replacing Miss Novak, Ford quit, leaving the vacancy to be filled by Kirk, who delighted Quine with his offer to have his own production company shoulder some of the burdens.

Since Kirk's company was now at the helm, or at least sharing it, Kirk in typical fashion took an authoritative role in the picture's creative process. But the film was intended as a star vehicle for Kim Novak, and she was not pleased at any changes he would have caused. According to film journalist Bill Davidson, she and Kirk fought on the set, with Novak telling Douglas how to play *his* scenes! Many directors have come unstuck trying to do that, but a sex symbol? Undoubtedly Miss Novak saw Kirk's attempts to change the script—which he undoubtedly saw as improving the film—as little more than temperamental interference. Richard Quine was stuck in the middle, producing the picture in partnership with Kirk yet in love with his leading lady. It proved to be a most unhappy experience, and certainly reinforced Kirk's determination to have greater creative control over any film which flew the Bryna banner.

EIGHT/
Spartacus

If starring in *Champion* had served to strengthen Kirk's aggression, then certainly portraying *Spartacus* enhanced his authoritative air. In the making of this twelve-million-dollar spectacle, Kirk was truly a General, much like Spartacus had been.

Generally believed by all other than historians to be a character of fiction, Spartacus actually lived, to the eternal chagrin of the Romans. A life-long slave sold like meat to the lanista (trainer) of a gladiatorial school, Spartacus led an army of gladiators and slaves in the great Servile War of 71 BC. He succeeded in smashing every army Rome sent out to combat them until his forces were caught between the legions of Pompey and Crassus. The slave army was defeated and the survivors were crucified along the Appian Way. The body of Spartacus lay somewhere on the battlefield, never to be identified.

Inspired by this incredible, true tale of courage, author Howard Fast mixed fact and fiction for his best-selling book *Spartacus*. Ironically, when Fast wrote his book he was an avowed communist and all major publishers refused to touch the novel, so Fast had to have the book published himself. His book was considered communist propaganda, the struggle of Spartacus against the Roman Empire depicting the plight of communist countries threatened by the Western world.

But by 1952 Fast had recanted his political affiliations and his book found favour with a major publisher. It went on to sell millions of copies all over the world. In America it was now seen to depict the free world's struggle to halt the spread of communism.

The truth of the matter is that Howard Fast's original concept was that *Spartacus* represented the struggle against oppression and wrong in whatever form it may come. And it was this concept which fired the imagination of Kirk Douglas. He authorized Edward Lewis, his right-hand-man and vice president of Bryna, to purchase the film rights. In the process Kirk promoted Lewis to movie producer for this epic production.

There was no way Kirk's little company could finance such a large-scale picture, which he and Lewis estimated would cost twelve million dollars, so they had to find a major studio to back them.

Expensive large-scale epics, particularly those depicting life in ancient times, had for a season, become big business. During the Fifties, Metro-Golwyn-Mayer had poured millions of dollars into two huge Roman epics, *Quo Vadis* and *Ben-Hur*, and both had taken fortunes. 20th Century-Fox had also delved into the past, treading ancient and biblical ground with pictures like *The Robe* and *The Egyptian*. But neither MGM nor Fox could afford to back *Spartacus*. Metro had only just recently completed *Ben-Hur*, and the fortune it was making in its initial release was to be ploughed straight into their planned remake of *Mutiny On The Bounty*. Fox, inspired by the immediate success of *Ben-Hur*, were wasting countless millions of dollars trying to make their *Cleopatra* the greatest epic ever.

Kirk was shrewd enough to turn to a major studio which was not renowned for making colossal productions, Universal. This was one place which had never won or lost on an epic, unlike most other studios, and with the tremendous success of *Ben-Hur* urging all the other major production companies to invest in lavish spectacles, Kirk was able to convince Universal to have a go. So Universal-International, as it was then called, agreed to put up the bulk of the huge budget which *Spartacus* required.

Although Universal was the paymaster general and Eddie Lewis the film's producer, Kirk acted as executive producer, which basically meant that he would ensure the picture would be made his way. However, he discovered along the way that he had to compromise, but overall *Spartacus* remained Kirk's picture because he was truly the General who superintended the production from start to finish.

To furnish a screenplay, Kirk commissioned Howard Fast to adapt his own book. The problem was, Fast was too close to his novel, which was structured in a totally unfilmable fashion. In the book the story of Spartacus is told in flashback and involves quite a number of characters, some who are involved only in the flashbacks, others who feature only in the post-war period of the novel. Fast was unable to satisfy Kirk and so Douglas had to turn to an experienced screenplaywright. In doing so, he walked straight into trouble.

The man he chose to write the screenplay was Dalton Trumbo. Trumbo had been blacklisted as a communist during the terrible witch-hunt which Kirk had openly opposed. Trumbo had been imprisoned after being sentenced for contempt of Congress when he refused to testify before the notorious House Un-American Activities Committee about his alleged membership of the Communist Party. During his time in jail at the Federal penitentiary, in Ashland, Trumbo had succeeded in secretly writing film scripts using various pseudonyms such as Sam Jackson and Robert Rich, and smuggling them out to be sold to movie makers on the black market. In 1956 his screenplay for *The Brave Won*, penned under the name of Robert Rich, won the Oscar. To the total embarrassment of the film industry, the elusive Robert Rich was unveiled as the outlawed Trumbo.

Kirk Douglas recognized Trumbo's talents as a writer and hired him to work with Fast. He even went as far as to announce in the film trade papers that Dalton Trumbo was writing the script for *Spartacus*. There was an outcry from the American Legion and the Motion Picture Alliance for the Preservation of American Ideals, who attacked the whole project of filming *Spartacus* as a communist plot. In picking two writers, Howard Fast and Dalton Trumbo, both of whom had been accused of communist affiliation, Kirk Douglas had suddenly earned for himself the enmity of communist haters.

To even suggest that Kirk was taking a stand either for or against communism in making *Spartacus* was farcical. To him the Servile War represented a neutral fight for survival. It was a principle which he, as a Jew, had grown up with. But he wanted his film to be more than just an expensive message. It was to be a supreme piece of screen entertainment and an exercise in producing not just a spectacle but an intelligent historical drama.

Universal stood by Kirk Douglas in his choice of writers. They were no longer members of The Motion Picture Association of America, the trade union of film producers. But they weren't intent on letting Kirk have it all his own way. They told him that Anthony Mann, who had directed many fine westerns for them, was to direct *Spartacus*. Kirk had misgivings about Mann, who undoubtedly had a flair for outdoors adventures as proven by his several James Stewart westerns such as *Where The River Bends* and *The Man From Laramie*. But *Spartacus* was not going to be a cowboys and Injuns story set in ancient Rome. But they were adamant, and so Kirk had no choice but to concede.

In choosing his cast, Kirk was truly ambitious. He did not want the usual run-of-the-mill Robert Taylor types who looked handsome enough in costume but lacked depth. He wanted the best actors that Universal's money could buy. The title role was no problem. Kirk himself had reserved that plum part for himself, which meant that there was no point in offering Charlton Heston any of the other roles since they were all secondary and certainly nowhere near as heroic. But the script did offer some excellent character roles.

Kirk sent off scripts to Laurence Olivier, Peter Ustinov and Charles Laughton. But in so doing he had Trumbo write different versions so that when Olivier, Ustinov and Laughton read their scripts, the characters each was being offered would seem to be of greater importance than the others. In this way Kirk succeeded in hooking Olivier, Ustinov and Laughton, who only discovered that their scripts were different when they actually arrived in Hollywood and compared scripts. For box office security, Kirk offered a small but important role to Tony Curtis, and another brief but equally vital part to John Gavin, who was then also a top star in America. The role of Varinia, the wife of Spartacus, went to a German girl, Sabina Bethman.

The picture was coming together and filled Kirk with a sense of excitement and enthusiasm which was almost unrestrained. He was into everything that was going on. He was hardly ever to be found in the large, five-roomed bungalow on the door of which hung the sign BRYNA PRODUCTIONS. It was from here that Eddie Lewis operated, but for Kirk the whole movie set was his office. He expended seemingly endless energy in over-seeing every department involved in the making of this movie. He spent hours with his production designer Alexander Golitzen as they worked out how they would plant vast walnut and citrus orchards along the San Fernando Valley, turning it into pre-Christian Italy; how they would build a Roman slum on the Universal backlot; how to transform the European street where Charles Laughton had once been hounded in *The Hunch-back Of Notre Dame* into the Roman Forum. Golitzen did nothing without full consultation with the General. The same was true with the art director, the wardrobe designer, the production manager, everybody. Kirk now had over ten thousand people working for him.

Filming began not in California, where the bulk of the film was to be shot, but in Spain, where Anthony Mann went to film the master shots of the final battle sequence. In recent years Spain had become a favourite location for makers of epic films, partly because the Spanish Army proved to be the most courageous film extras when it came to filming huge battle sequences. About 8,000 volunteers were recruited from the Spanish infantry to portray Roman soldiers engaged in compli-cated and authentic manoeuvres of cohorts, maniples and cen-turies.

It was while the forces of Spartacus and the legions of Rome were fighting it out on a vast plain situated some forty kilometres from Madrid that another fight was ensuing be-tween Anthony Mann and his employers. Kirk was at the fore-front of the on-set battle which resulted in him firing Mann from the picture. Certainly Kirk was not happy with Mann's work, but neither were Universal, according to Kirk who told me, 'We started shooting with Anthony Mann directing, but I didn't think he was right for this picture. Universal, who put up the money, insisted on using him. But after the first week they said, "Kirk, you were right. *You've* got to get rid of him."

'So *I* had to tell Anthony, who was a very nice guy, that we had to get somebody else.'

None of the stars on the picture witnessed what went on in

Spain because none of them, except for Kirk, went out there. Tony Curtis said, 'I never worked with Tony Mann on the picture. But I could see Kirk and Universal just didn't like the way the work was coming out. I met Anthony Mann before the film started. Then they went off on location and when they came back he wasn't around anymore.'

Now Kirk felt he had the chance to get the kind of director he thought could really give *Spartacus* some class. He nominated Stanley Kubrick and Universal agreed.

It was a life-saving job for Kubrick who had been working endlessly with Marlon Brando on *One-Eyed Jacks*, a western which Brando was to produce and star in and Kubrick was to direct. Brando ended up firing Kubrick and directed the film himself with disastrous results. Kirk sent a copy of the script to Kubrick who, according to Douglas, said, 'I'd love to do it,' and was on the set of *Spartacus* a week later.

One of his first acts as director was to suggest that they replace Sabina Bethman with Jean Simmons. Kirk thought it a wonderful idea and so Jean Simmons joined the cast complete with her own costume designer, Bill Thomas.

If making *The Vikings* had been a headache for Kirk, then *Spartacus* was like a blinding migraine. But throughout every crisis, he was like a dynamic force which just refused to go under. He stayed on top of everything. The only time he was literally floored was when he was hit midway through production by a virus which had him out of the picture for ten days, the first time in his career that he ever missed work due to illness. Tony Curtis was also thrown out of work for four weeks when he split his Achilles' tendon one Sunday afternoon when playing tennis on Kirk's private court.

Such traumas forced the schedule to be changed constantly. The biggest problem arose when Jean Simmons fell ill and had to undergo surgery. Kirk was informed by the medics that she would be out of action for a month. The trouble was, she still had her scenes with Olivier to film and he was due back at Stratford-on-Avon in England for appearances in Shakespearean repertory. Kirk and Eddie Lewis made frantic transAtlantic calls in an effort to extend Olivier's stay in Hollywood, but Stratford would only allow one week's grace. In one final desperate manoeuvre, Kirk coaxed the medics to allow Jean to complete her scenes with Olivier under a doctor's supervision, allowing Olivier to finish his part and leave after the one allotted extra week.

Rescheduling was far from being Kirk's biggest challenge. He had a falling out with two of his most vital allies, Charles Laughton and Stanley Kubrick.

Kirk was totally unaware that Laughton was about to rebel and virtually walk off the picture because of anything that he had done. So it came as a tremendous shock when Laughton flatly refused to continue filming. He virtually accused Kirk Douglas of being a collaborator with Laurence Olivier in a plot to undermine Laughton's role.

The fact was that Laurence Olivier, a master of persuasion, had been gradually improving on his own role of Crassus by making casual suggestions to Kirk Douglas and Stanley Kubrick on the set. If there was any one actor Kirk Douglas was in awe of, it was Olivier, and he allowed him to rewrite his lines. Peter Ustinov, who knew of Olivier's knack of gentle persuasion, would watch the master in action with Kirk and the director, and was amused by it. But when Charles Laughton saw what was happening, he concluded that Olivier and Douglas were bent on enhancing Olivier's role specifically to belittle Laughton's. It was simply a neurosis of Laughton's, but one which had him storming off in a tantrum. Nothing which Kirk or Kubrick could say would placate the hefty actor.

In desperation, Kirk turned to Ustinov for help. Ustinov had become very friendly with Laughton and was just about the only person Laughton trusted. Ustinov suggested that he and Laughton be allowed to rewrite all their own scenes, to which Kirk agreed. From then on Ustinov and Laughton worked long into each night, rewriting their scenes, inventing some of the wittiest dialogue in the whole picture.

But placating Charles Laughton did not end Kirk's problems. The director himself began accusing Douglas of undermining *his* authority, refusing him the artistic control he wanted. Certainly Kirk was intent on having the picture made his way, but he was willing to compromise on some things. Conferences were called between Kirk, Kubrick, Lewis and Trumbo. Poor Trumbo had not had it easy with this film. After falling out with Howard Fast he had been left to complete the mammoth script himself. He had written a total of seven complete script revisions which ultimately totalled 1,534 pages and over 250,000 words.

Kirk was satisfied with the script as it now was and was unwilling to keep changing it. He had allowed Olivier, Ustinov and Laughton to make their own contributions, but any major changes at this stage seemed out of the question. It's a sad fact that despite Kubrick's contribution to *Spartacus*, which undoubtedly was a major factor in the final and brilliant result, Kubrick today virtually disowns the picture, claiming that it was hardly his film because Kirk Douglas was so unbending.

Douglas, however, defends his position thus:

> Kubrick was working for one year with Marlon Brando on *One-Eyed Jacks* while I was preparing *Spartacus*. I had worked a long time on the script with Dalton Trumbo and we worked very hard getting the right cast.
>
> I showed [Kubrick] the script of *Spartacus*. He said, 'I'd love to do it,' and the next week I brought him over and introduced him to the cast and he started. We had many discussions with Trumbo about the script, and Stanley was in on everything. But when he came into the picture it had been cast and the script had been done, and he *did* bring about a lot of changes.
>
> All of this is by way of saying the ego of film makers is a very frustrating thing. It's hard for any one person to say 'It's *my* picture. *I* did it all.' I know that in Europe they have a tendency to lose the writer's name on the credit titles. Suppose I was a great director and I did *Macbeth* and way down somewhere it said, 'By William Shakespeare.' You need a writer, so I think the frustrating thing in movie making unlike a painting or a book is that you can't say, 'I did it all.' I don't care who they are, because you need so many other elements.
>
> I thought Stanley did a brilliant job directing *Spartacus*. He made a lot of changes. The whole concept of the love scene at the beginning was originally a dialogue scene. But all the dialogue was taken out and it was done visually. And that was Kubrick's concept. It was brilliant and I'm the first to say it.

Jean Simmons recognized what a difficult task Kubrick had, and indeed she shows neutrality over the controversy, owing much to both Kubrick and Douglas.

'It was very difficult for Stanley Kubrick,' she once told me, 'because he came on at the last minute so he had no preparation with the script. He was shooting from pages that were coming in every day. We were never quite sure what was going to happen. But when Stanley came on he said he would like me to do it, and Kirk seemed to be happy about that.'

The cast members certainly seemed aware of the difficulty Kubrick was experiencing but the general feeling does seem to be that he made his mark on the film.

Tony Curtis said, 'They held a line on Stanley a lot; Kirk, Eddie Lewis and Universal. But Stanley in his own inimitable manner was able to say, "No, I don't like that. I'd like to try this." And he'd get it his way. But it wasn't an easy task because he was dealing with Kirk who was running the company and wanted to make sure the picture was made on his terms because he had a lot at stake. But Stanley I think gave that film a style it wouldn't have had if someone else had directed it.'

Not all, though, who worked on the film found Kirk to be flexible. There were definitely times when he did become too self-indulgent if only because he wanted to ensure that what was captured on film was what he wanted. Yakima Canutt, the famed stuntman and action director, discovered this when he was hired to stage some ferocious action sequences on the terrain of Thousand Oaks, California. Since all the master footage of the battle had been done in Spain, it was Canutt's job to work with the individual actors to make their involvement look as realistic as possible. The following is from Canutt's autobiography, *Stunt Man*, which relates to his association with Kirk Douglas on *Spartacus*:

> During my work on the battle, the director sent Tony Curtis to our location so that I could do his scenes in the fighting. Tony was a fine actor and very cooperative, and we got some good scenes.
>
> I also did a number of scenes with John Ireland, who was also very cooperative. I did moving shots with him in

battle, and he handled his sword well, and his death scene was excellent.

One day the star, Kirk Douglas, came to do some close fighting shots. I had worked out what I thought was a good routine for him and had his personal stunt man run through the scene for him. When the routine finished, Kirk shook his head in disapproval.

'Naw, naw,' he said, 'here is what we'll do.'

Then he started showing the stunt man another routine. I knew, or at least had heard, that Kirk had a lot of his own money in the picture, so all I did was holler 'action' and 'cut.' When he finished and left I started another sequence.

After work the following day we saw the rushes in the studio projection room. When they finished Kirk turned to me. 'Those scenes of mine are not good,' he said. 'I should have had scenes like the ones you shot with Curtis and Ireland. They looked great.'

'Curtis and Ireland took direction,' I replied pointedly, and that ended the conversation. I might add, I never worked for Kirk again. But there is one thing I have to admit about Kirk Douglas. He is really a fine actor.

If Kirk is one to push, then he certainly pushes no one harder than himself. This was fully illustrated when it came to filming the thrilling gladiatorial combat between Spartacus and Draba, played by Woody Strode. The script was brief and to the point in its description of the scene.

> Draba and Spartacus face each other and cross their weapons. The fight begins. Spartacus, armed with the short Thracian sword, has little chance against Draba and his trident. The combat comes to a climax when Draba downs Spartacus, places the trident against his throat.

Working with a crew of veteran stuntmen, Kirk had those few lines expanded into eight pages detailing the movements of the characters which the stuntmen fully expected to undertake themselves. But Kirk insisted that he and Strode perform the choreographed fight scene themselves without the use of doubles. There followed two weeks of rehearsals as Douglas and Strode worked out the hairy routine while the stuntmen stood to the side as spectators. It took twelve days actually to film the sequence which lasts just seven minutes on the screen. The watching stuntmen agreed that it was the most dangerous screen fight they had ever seen.

Kirk Douglas is all things to all men. To those who like to do their job themselves, he is interfering and difficult. To those who welcome participation, he is a motivating force. As far as *Spartacus* is concerned, it remains Kirk Douglas's crowning achievement as a film maker. The film's brilliance stems from the fact that Kirk picked the right people for the job. It bears his hallmark, even as movies once bore the stamps of Selznick, Goldwyn and Thalberg.

As an actor, *Spartacus* is a performance for which Kirk should receive the recognition he deserves. As with *The Bad And The Beautiful*, Kirk didn't have to worry about showing his strength, because you knew it was there. What he did have to do was portray emotion and charm. Spartacus was probably the first character Kirk played on screen which people had to love. And his death scene probably marks the first time anybody ever cried at the demise of a Kirk Douglas character.

There were no personal Oscars for Douglas for *Spartacus*. But the film did win four Oscars for Best Supporting Actor (Ustinov), Best Colour Cinematography (Russell Metty), Best Art Direction (Eric Orbom) shared with Best Set Decoration (Russell A. Gausman and Julia Heron), and Best Costume Design (Bill Thomas, Valles and Peruzzi). Those four Academy Awards belong equally to Kirk Douglas.

When the film opened it was an immediate hit. The critics acclaimed it as one of the most intelligent and moving epics ever made, and the futile efforts of the American Legion and the Motion Picture Alliance to picket theatres where it was shown were to no avail.

The film really made Stanley Kubrick, who went on to make classics like *Dr Strangelove*, *2001: A Space Odyssey* and *A Clockwork Orange*. But because of his own personal feelings towards *Spartacus*, many members of the public aren't even aware that he directed it. But they always remember the film for Kirk Douglas.

'I'm rather proud of *Spartacus*,' Kirk told me. 'It's difficult to make a big epic picture in which the characters stand out, and I think the actors dominated the film.'

His last word on the matter was, 'Stanley Kubrick directed it brilliantly.'

NINE/
/Lonely Are The Brave

When Kirk Douglas was still on Broadway and movies were less than a twinkle in his eye, he took his mother to a theatre where he was appearing. He showed her his name, visible to all as it spread over a big marquee.

He pointed up.

'Mama, one day your name will be up there in lights too,' he told her.

She just laughed it off as a joke.

When *Spartacus* opened in Los Angeles, Bryna Danielovitch was Kirk's most important guest at the lavish premiere. Undaunted by the ignored pickets from the anti-communist groups there to show their outrage over the Dalton Trumbo affair, Kirk stood his mother before the cinema and told her to look up at the marquee. There she read the words, 'A Bryna Production'. When she had first come to America she had not even been able to write her own name. It was Kirk who later taught her. Later still he had promised to put his mother's name up in lights.

Now there it was, her name lit up like an ensign which Kirk was proudly proclaiming to the world. It gave him just about the biggest thrill of his life just to see his mother's expression of wonder and pride.

Universal were just as thrilled because in its initial release, *Spartacus* grossed more than fourteen million dollars domestically, and a lot more than that worldwide. At the outset of the

89

mammoth project, they were willing to pour a great deal of money into Kirk's ambitious production, but they needed some kind of guarantee to offset the enormous risk they were taking. The best guarantee Kirk could offer was himself, to make a series of films for the studio over the next few years but non-exclusively. Kirk wasn't about to be tied down by another studio contract and become the sole property of anyone other than himself.

Straight after *Spartacus*, Kirk was back on the Universal lot with another Bryna production and another western, *The Last Sunset*. Kirk found himself in a rather curious position because Universal's own star property Rock Hudson was to take top billing, giving Kirk only second place in the credits.

The film didn't prove to be one of Kirk's better westerns, although it featured an intriguing plot for a horse opera. Kirk played a drifter pursued by lawman Hudson whose brother-in-law was murdered by Douglas. The two eventually become contenders for the charms of Dorothy Malone, with whom Douglas has had an affair in the past. As Hudson succeeds in winning the affections of the lady, Douglas becomes attracted to her teenage daughter, played by Carol Lynley. The crux of the matter is that Lynley turns out to be Kirk's own daughter, adding some immoral spice to an otherwise routine western.

The screenplay was again by Dalton Trumbo, who attempted to give some dimension to the stereotyped characters, but it is a script which Trumbo was not particularly proud of. Edward Lewis was again producing, although this time in partnership with Eugene Frenke, but as with *Spartacus* Kirk was still the man in charge. And again this led to conflicts.

Attempting to direct *The Last Sunset* was Robert Aldrich, a man who was generally used to directing films which he also produced. He was not happy with the way *The Last Sunset* turned out because he felt it was hardly his film. Like Stanley Kubrick the year before, Aldrich was in contention with Kirk Douglas. Kubrick of course had still been something of a beginner and made his name with *Spartacus*, but Aldrich had been around for some time and had a number of successes to his name, such as *Vera Cruz* and *The Big Knife*.

He describes *The Last Sunset* as one of his 'real bad pictures'.

'There's no doubt that my work as a director is much better if there isn't a producer,' he says. 'When there's a producer you get into those inevitable conflicts of how much a sequence costs and who should be in the picture—and I don't want that noise.'

But that was precisely the noise heard on the set of *The Last Sunset*. The main problem was trying to direct Kirk in a film that was basically his own. Aldrich describes Kirk's behaviour while making the film as 'impossible'. The one redeeming feature for Aldrich was working with Rock Hudson who, he says, was a pleasure to work with. Part of the problem with this picture was that although Kirk condescended to being billed second to Rock Hudson, he was intent on being the star of the picture, and in true form he dominated it both on screen and off. Aldrich's headache wasn't just that he was dealing with a temperamental star about whom he could talk to his producers, because the producers were hired by Kirk. So he did his job as best he could, and when it was in the can, he simply got on with his next job as a director while Kirk started thinking about his next production for Bryna.

Edward Lewis had purchased the screen rights to a book called *Brave Cowboy* about a modern-day cowboy hanging on to the defunct code of the cowboys. Kirk turned the story over to Dalton Trumbo to fashion into a screenplay. While Trumbo worked hard at his typewriter on the script for what would be called *Lonely Are The Brave*, Kirk returned to Europe to film a German-American co-production, *Town Without Pity*.

This time Kirk wasn't in charge. The picture was produced and directed by German film maker Gottfried Reinhardt, who several years earlier had directed Kirk in *The Story Of Three Loves*. *Town Without Pity* proved to be somewhat pretentious though obviously sincere in its depiction of a military trial at which four American GIs are accused of raping a German girl, played by sixteen-year-old Christine Kaufmann. Kirk Douglas plays the Army lawyer who handles the defence.

For once Kirk was able to concentrate more on his acting rather than anything else, and despite the film's failure to fulfil its potential, the courtroom scenes did give Kirk the chance to deliver a fine performance, portraying a man who is restrained and compassionate yet quite terrifying when angry.

The film was not a critical or box office success, but it kept Kirk busy until he was able to begin making what proved to be one of his own personal favourites, *Lonely Are The Brave*.

For tax reasons, Kirk chose to create a brand new production company and called it 'Joel' after his son. And so for a while Bryna was put to rest while Joel took up the gauntlet to make the films Kirk wanted to do. *Lonely Are The Brave* in particular was a picture he felt he had to make, even though it seemed hardly viable as a commercial film. The character Kirk played, a cowboy who breaks out of jail and heads for the hills, is doomed to lose. And losers rarely if ever make for good box office. But with Universal eager for another Kirk Douglas picture, he was able to get the show on the road, only this time he didn't pick a distinguished director to helm a picture which Kirk clearly wanted made in a certain way. Instead he chose David Miller, an experienced director but one whose films were hardly in the big league. *Lonely Are The Brave* presented Miller with an opportunity to develop some style, and indeed he turned the climactic lengthy mountain chase into a unique piece of cinema.

Eddie Lewis was still Kirk's right-hand man in the production office and Kirk was once more involved in every aspect of the production. He even hired his son Michael, now seventeen, to assist Leon Barsha in editing the film. The editing-room must have been a very crowded place for quite a few weeks with David Miller, Leon Basha, Michael Douglas and the boss all cutting and snipping at 35mm film. The final results came out pretty much as Kirk had hoped they would. It presented a man much after Kirk's own heart who nose-thumbed the system. Kirk had always striven to be his own man, living on his own terms, and that's exactly what the hero of *Lonely Are The Brave* tried to do.

'It happens to be a point of view I love,' he says. 'This is what attracted me to the story—the difficulty of being an individual today. Life gets more and more complex and convoluted. Young people are not happy with what's going on, and they're right. The character in *Lonely Are The Brave* had that quality. He didn't want to belong to this day and age. It's difficult to buck the system. That's the tragedy of it.'

It wasn't always easy for Kirk to buck the system either. When he presented *Lonely Are The Brave* to Universal as a finished picture, they took one look at it and wondered what to do with it. They had thought it would be a lively contemporary cowboy picture. Now they found they had a picture with subtle qualities about it. But what to do with it? Deciding that they couldn't possibly present it as a commercial piece, they tried to present it as an 'arty' picture. The film was a failure, and Kirk blamed the studio. 'This has much to do with the way the studio presented and distributed it,' he says. 'They looked upon it as being not very commercial, and the way they handled it made it exactly that.'

Once again Kirk Douglas was finding that successful pictures were not so easy to come by. His previous two pictures had been flops and there would be a few more to come. But if nothing else, he can take comfort in the fact that *Lonely Are The Brave* has become something of a classic, and is today studied in cinema courses in colleges and universities in America, joining the ranks of other box office disasters like *Lust For Life*, *Paths Of Glory* and *Ace In The Hole*, all of which have earned far more in critical appraisal than in box office receipts.

In search of a success, Kirk let himself be talked into making *Two Weeks In Another Town*, an attempt by MGM virtually to copy and repeat the glories they'd enjoyed a decade earlier with *The Bad And The Beautiful*. John Houseman was again producing, Vincente Minnelli directed and Charles Schnee wrote the script.

This time the setting wasn't Hollywood but Rome, which, in 1962 when the film was made, was enjoying the status of the movie mecca of Europe. Based on an Irwin Shaw novel, the film told of a once-big star, played by Douglas, who after recovering from a nervous breakdown, flies out to Italy to play a bit part in a movie being directed by an old friend, Edward G. Robinson. When Robinson falls ill, Douglas takes over direction of the picture.

The film features lots of film folk who are complex, unlikeable and parasitic. There is the ex-wife, played by Cyd Charisse, who still tries to possess Douglas; the young American actor, played by George Hamilton, who despises his director; the director's wife who accuses him of having an affair with an Italian starlet, played by Rosanna Schiaffino. The only real endearing character is a beautiful Italian girl, played by Dahlia Lavi, who falls for Douglas.

The movie is probably best known for its use of footage from *The Bad And The Beautiful* seen when Robinson and Douglas take a glimpse of one of their earlier triumphs. But somehow using that sequence from the classic simply made one realize how inferior *Two Weeks In Another Town* actually was.

Kirk contends that the film was basically ruined by a studio executive who decided to re-edit the film to make it more palatable for family audiences, and he admits that both he and Minnelli were disappointed with the story although they did enjoy the opportunity to work with each other again. But if they had at any time ever thought that they had the makings of a good film, then Edward G. Robinson was under no delusions. He hated the script and was unenthusiastic about both the film and his own part. Kirk, on the other hand, is hardly ever unenthusiastic about any part he plays. And that is his amazing ability. He can get stuck into the most meagre of screenplays and try and do something worth while with it. If his reputation for being awkward has tarnished his image within the industry, then his enthusiasm and total enjoyment for his work are the qualities—his evident talent aside—which have maintained his stature as a major Hollywood star.

All this in retrospect can make Kirk justifiably proud of his track record, but back in 1963 he could find little to boast about. He had not had a hit since *Spartacus*, three years before. *The Hook* was not the solution.

Attempting to deal with a moral issue, *The Hook* was set during the Korean War with Douglas typically playing a hard-nosed sergeant. After taking prisoners, Douglas and his men are ordered to shoot them. Douglas is visibly shocked at the order but proceeds to carry it out. But one of his men, played by Robert Walker, refuses to obey. That is the substance of this war drama, which then proceeds to examine the individual men involved. It failed both to be thought provoking, as was *Paths Of Glory*, or to be a serious though action-packed war drama. So not many people bothered going to see it.

Suddenly Kirk couldn't do anything right, seemingly. He

tried his hand at comedy again in *For Love Or Money*. It was a fairly routine exercise with Kirk playing an attorney who is hired by wealthy Thelma Ritter to act as matchmaker for her three lovely daughters, Mitzi Gaynor, Leslie Parish and Julie Newmar, as if any three rich beauties would have such trouble. Of course Douglas and Gaynor fall for each other, and the film ends with a triple wedding. Not surprisingly, Kirk himself was disappointed with the film, though not with one line from a review of the film by tough American film critic Judith Crist, who wrote, 'Kirk Douglas proves himself an expert with a fast line and a comic situation.'

But Kirk wasn't laughing. He needed a commercial hit, so he turned all his efforts towards making one. It was *The List Of Adrian Messenger*, a whodunit made for Kirk's Joel company. Eddie Lewis again stood right behind Kirk as his producer, but this time Kirk wanted a director he felt he could trust to turn out a polished production. He chose John Huston. He also persuaded Huston to take a small role in the film as a huntsman, which was just fine with Huston because, being an Irish resident, he knew much about the British landed gentry and about the Irish aristocrats' love of fox hunting which was featured to grand effect in the movie.

The star of the picture was George C. Scott as a retired British intelligence officer who is given a list of names by his friend Adrian Messenger who asks him to check on them. One by one, beginning with Messenger, the people on the list are murdered, and the culprit is none other than Kirk Douglas, who takes the best role in the film while submitting to what amounted to rock-bottom billing.

Kirk got pretty much the kind of picture he had hoped for from Huston. Perhaps surprisingly, considering the fiery temperaments of both Huston and Douglas, the two worked amicably enough. Douglas particularly enjoyed the opportunity to hide behind various disguises for his part. One evening he even arrived home wearing one of his several masks. Peter and Eric were baffled by the stranger, but Anne wasn't fooled for a minute, to Kirk's disappointment.

Between them, Kirk and John Huston concocted a second guessing game for the benefit of the film's audience. They hired a number of top stars and disguised them heavily. When the film was finished the story's narrator reveals the famous faces hidden by the masks. There was Frank Sinatra as a gypsy, Burt Lancaster as an anti-fox-hunting suffragette, Robert Mitchum as a crippled old man and Tony Curtis as an organ-grinder. Tony was now such a close friend of Kirk's that when Tony married Christine Kaufman in February of 1963, Kirk was best man and Anne was matron of honour.

Despite the quality that was up there on the screen, *The List Of Adrian Messenger* was not a success. With the exception of one more film in 1964, it was to be the end of Kirk Douglas's own personal productions until the end of the decade. It was a situation which could have driven Kirk into the depths of despair if it hadn't been for a single incident.

Kirk was on his way to his second house in Palm Springs. He was sleeping in the back of his car while his chauffeur took the wheel. Somewhere along the route the chauffeur stopped for reasons best known to himself, and got out of the car. Kirk awoke and also got out to stretch his legs.

The chauffeur returned and thinking the boss was still silently dozing on the back seat, he drove off. Kirk suddenly found himself stranded in the middle of nowhere, and to add to his embarrassment, he didn't have a dime on him. He had to hitch a lift.

He suddenly thought, 'I'm right back where I started.' At first he felt frightened, but then he experienced what he describes as 'a cynical amusement about the whole deal'.

He says on reflection, 'I guess it suddenly gave me a sense of balance. And I needed that.'

TEN / A Hero of Telemark, Israel and Washington

Kirk has always loved his country. He is proud of his patriotism and has never forgotten that while he has achieved everything virtually on his own, it was only because of the system which America has adopted that he was allowed to get the education he enjoyed and enter into the profession which he chose. He had always felt that he owed his country something, and so in 1963 it came as a great honour for him personally when President Kennedy requisitioned him as an official goodwill ambassador for the United States State Department.

Throughout 1963 he was touring numerous South American countries, the object being to promote a better understanding of Northern America. Anne accompanied him as he met with heads of state. He also addressed teachers and professors of education and student bodies. Kirk took particular joy in meeting with students, and over the years in his capacity as a goodwill ambassador, he has met with students all round the world.

There were other aspects to this period of his life, however.

As well as the goodwill he was spreading, Kirk was also enjoying a break from movie making, giving him time to breathe and assess his position in the film world. He'd had seven flops in a row now, all of which had been made in the brief span of just three years. He felt it was time to stretch his acting wings a bit and return to the place he had started—the theatre. Kirk told me:

> I wanted at that time to do something different. I still thought I was primarily a stage actor. I bought a book called 'One Flew Over The Cuckoo's Nest', which is a classic now and is studied in Universities. I had a play developed out of it and took it on Broadway. I had some good actors in it. I had Gene Wilder, for instance, who was just starting. I had William Daniels. It was a damned good play but the critics didn't know how to deal with it. It was ahead of its time. I played in it for about five months to a mild reception from the critics. But audiences always responded to it.
>
> I remember saying to my wife, 'This is a classic, but they just don't know it yet.'
>
> Of course, since then it's played off Broadway in many places over many years, and it's studied. And my son, Michael, who always loved it, took it over and he produced it as a film.

It's ironic that for several years Kirk tried to get *One Flew Over The Cuckoo's Nest* made into a film, and it was finally Michael Douglas who actually achieved that. But back in 1963 it was a play that was far too frank and daring for the screen.

Like most actors who have worked in both the cinema and on the stage, Kirk didn't find the theatre exactly lucrative. He had to make another film and in 1964 he finally struck gold with *Seven Days In May*. It was a taut, brilliant military drama with Burt Lancaster playing an American general who sets up a secret base in the desert, unbeknownst to the President, played by Fredric March. It is Lancaster's aide, played by Douglas, who discovers the secret base and exposes Lancaster.

The film was put together by Joel and Seven Arts, and produced by Edward Lewis. It was Kirk's film and, as before, he exerted all the authority he could muster over it, much to the disdain of the film's director, John Frankenheimer.

Frankenheimer is himself a rather aggressive man and very outspoken. He didn't like Kirk Douglas. He didn't like the way he was trying to direct every scene himself. He didn't like the way he argued and fought with Frankenheimer. According to Frankenheimer, Kirk was jealous of Lancaster, stating, 'Kirk wanted to be Burt Lancaster—he's wanted to be Burt Lancaster all his life.' That statement sounds more like sour grapes than a statement of fact, because if ever there was a Hollywood actor who wanted to be a complete individual, it was Kirk Douglas. However, it is feasible to suggest that because Burt had been enjoying continuing success while Kirk had been having one failure after another, he may well have been jealous of Lancaster's success. One thing was sure, the two actors were still close friends.

Their friendship, though, was put to the test. Kirk was keyed up to virtually direct every scene he was in. Whenever Lancaster had a scene with Kirk, he found himself in the rather subordinate position of being told how to play his part by Douglas. By this time Lancaster had cooled his fiery temperament. Kirk had gone from strength to strength in his capacity as a film producer, and ever since *Spartacus* he had been used to giving the orders. Probably what Kirk really looked for was not total control over any one film but a compromise between himself and the director. Few directors were willing to make such compromises. John Frankenheimer wasn't prepared but since Kirk was technically producing the picture, it was difficult to challenge and oppose him.

Burt Lancaster allowed Kirk to direct him because he admired Douglas immensely for his courageous stand in openly using Dalton Trumbo's name during the making of *Spartacus*. So Burt grinned his toothy grin, and just got on with the job.

Kirk was now showing courage in his choice of subject in making *Seven Days In May*. It was a story few others would have dared to touch. The idea that a general could lead a revolt against the President of America was at the time very sensitive, especially considering that the general's motive is his abhorrence of what he sees as the appeasement of the Soviet Union by a pacifist American President. President John F. Kennedy knew about the film and is on record as saying that he felt the film should be made. Tragically, he didn't live to see it.

It certainly wasn't an easy film to find financing for. Kirk and his partner Lewis had managed to capture the interest of John

Frankenheimer, who had just completed the political thriller *The Manchurian Candidate*, which in itself was another touchy subject. Once Frankenheimer had agreed to direct the film, Burt Lancaster, who had worked with Frankenheimer on *The Young Savages* and *The Birdman of Alcatraz*, gave in to Kirk's persuasion to star in it. With the interest of Seven Arts captured, Kirk and Eddie Lewis strengthened their project by casting the very prestigious Fredric March, and also by encouraging screen goddess Ava Gardner back to the screen for the first time in six years. Kirk finally had a 2,200,000-dollar budget to work with, and the film swung into action.

Although there was no active cooperation from the Pentagon in making the film, when Frankenheimer needed to shoot a riot sequence right outside of the White House, the President's Press Secretary Pierre Salinger arranged for the President to be at Hyannisport, allowing the scene to be filmed without interference for either President Kennedy or the film unit. Salinger also allowed Kirk and his cohorts to tour the President's office and other rooms in the White House so that they could be duplicated authentically in the studio.

The realism, the controversial subject, the sharp direction, the flawless performances and the dedication of Kirk Douglas all resulted in a film which the critics lauded and the public flocked to see. It was an undisputed hit.

During 1964 Kirk's friendship with President Kennedy had flourished. The two men had certainly met and discussed the film during its making, and also in that year Kennedy sent Kirk and his wife off once more to promote their country, this time in the Far East. The year 1964 had succeeded in enforcing Kirk's reputation as an actor, a producer, an American, and perhaps more than anything else, as one of Hollywood's most unlikeable characters. It was a time when he was even actively promoting his difficult yet highly saleable image.

'Virtue is not photogenic,' he said, not for the last time. 'What is it to be a nice guy? To be nothing, that's what. A big fat zero with a smile for everybody. I'm probably the most disliked actor in Hollywood, and I feel pretty good about it. Because that's *me*. I'm a pretty unlikeable character, to tell you the truth.

'Me, I'm a sonofabitch. Plain and simple. Why try to act the nice guy?'

Now, more than any other time, Kirk Douglas was receiving world recognition as the off-screen bad guy of Hollywood. In years to come it would become something of a joke to him, but during the Sixties, the very mention of Kirk Douglas as a potential member of any film's cast was enough to give movie directors sleepless nights.

One such man was Elliot Silverstein, a thirty-seven-year-old newcomer who was given the daunting task of directing the now classic comedy western, *Cat Ballou*. He'd made only one film prior to that, but the producers and Columbia Studios had enough faith in him to give him the task of filming the tale of Cat Ballou and Kid Shelleen, having already turned down some two dozen other directors. Jane Fonda had been signed for the title role, but the part of Kid Shelleen still had to be filled. The producers wanted Kirk Douglas. When Silverstein learned that, he was struck with panic. *Cat Ballou* was only Silverstein's second picture, but his first *major* film, and he had heard all the stories about how Kirk Douglas gave his directors hell. The young director didn't think he'd be able to handle the veteran Hollywood trouble-maker.

He begged the Columbia brass to reconsider and assign some other actor to the role. But they were adamant. And it was up to Silverstein, they said, to make sure that Douglas accepted the role. They made him promise to call Kirk, who had already been sent a script, and do his best to persuade Douglas to take the film. With much trepidation, Silverstein made the phone call to Kirk's Beverly Hills home. It turned out to be a long conversation during which time Silverstein did his utmost to convince Douglas he was perfect for the part, even though he hoped against hope that Kirk would refuse it.

Eventually Kirk told him, 'To be honest with you, the role of Kid Shelleen isn't large enough for me, or small enough for a cameo.'

Silverstein breathed a sigh of relief, and told himself, 'I'm off the hook!'

Instead of Kirk Douglas, Elliot Silverstein ended up with the greatest hellraiser since Errol Flynn, Lee Marvin!

Kid Shelleen is one of many parts Kirk turned down which in retrospect could have been further highlights in his already notable career. Among the other roles he declined was Patton in the film which gave George C. Scott an Oscar. 'I turned down both *Cat Ballou* and *Patton*,' Kirk once told me, 'and the actors who took both parts won Oscars. So *I'm* not so smart.' One thing was sure. Kirk was still in demand. *Seven Days In May* had been particularly effective in presenting Kirk as a military man, and undoubtedly because of this, Kirk's next batch of films would all feature him as a man at war.

His next choice of picture was a somewhat curious one. It was *In Harm's Way*, an epic saga about the war in the South Pacific, beginning with the attack on Pearl Harbor. It was a curious choice for Kirk in two ways. First of all, it was produced and directed by Otto Preminger, himself a man with a reputation for being a task master who would take no bull from any actor. Secondly, the real star of the picture was John Wayne, and when all was said and done, *In Harm's Way* was a John Wayne picture, not a Kirk Douglas one. Wayne played a naval captain who gets put behind a desk when he fails in his first assignment right after Pearl Harbor. But being John Wayne, his talents to command become evident and he is put in charge of an important naval campaign which, of course, he succeeds in. Douglas played Wayne's second in command, whose flirty wife is killed in the attack on Pearl Harbor, and whose growing bitterness leads him to rape Jill Hayworth, who plays the girlfriend of Brandon De Wilde who plays the son of John Wayne!

Despite the contrived plot, the film featured a number of magnificently staged battle sequences, including the attack on Pearl Harbor. During the filming of this scene, Douglas and Wayne stood to one side as the film's hardware took all the honours. Japanese old-type, single-engine planes dived towards the harbour, buzzing over the extras portraying sun seekers. Deafening explosions shook the whole western end of Honolulu where the film was based, and buildings were blown to bits. Standing near Douglas, Wayne was taking photographs of the events that were being recreated for the screen. 'Goddam it!' Wayne said. 'That sure was something. I hope they had some film running in that camera,' he added pointing towards a

Panavision camera mounted on a van protected by wire mesh which dashed through the exploding set.

Inside the van was Otto Preminger, proving he had courage as well as talent. This was the kind of heroics one would normally expect from Kirk Douglas or John Wayne. But there are few directors as tough and uncompromising as Preminger. It wouldn't have been at all surprising to find Douglas and Preminger in conflict, or Douglas and Wayne, or even Wayne with Preminger. But despite the occasional explosions by both the naval hardware and Preminger on the set when someone was incompetent enough to arouse his considerable anger, the Hawaiian islands were relatively peaceful during the film unit's stay.

While the rest of the cast and crew were given suites in the island's biggest hotel, the Ilikai, Kirk Douglas opted for a separate residence, and Preminger obliged by paying his rent for a villa near Diamond Head where he could stay with his entire family who came out to be with him and enjoy the Hawaiian sunshine. He had found a new hobby, which helped him to relax when he had days off from the gruelling task of making this picture. He discovered surfing. He'd never tried it before, but he took lessons and became quite adept at it.

When Kirk was on the film's set, it was hard work. But because it was basically Wayne's film, he found plenty of time just to be with his family and surf.

'It's a long haul, all right,' he said at the time. 'But I'm enjoying it. How can you fail to enjoy yourself in surroundings like these?'

He had five months to enjoy his surroundings, being the time spent making the picture. A staggering six million dollars were poured into its making, which was then an awesome amount for a film shot in black and white.

The film gave Kirk the opportunity to get to know John Wayne a little better, being the first of three films he would make with the elder statesman of Hollywood. Despite their political differences—Kirk's a Democrat and Wayne was a Republican—there was a special chemistry between them on the set, and they had tremendous respect for each other. But there was little socializing between them after shooting hours. Wayne was the kind of man who liked to be with his pals, drinking well into the night with them. But Kirk was at this time of his life more content to be with his family. The only thing that kept him away from Anne and the boys at the end of a day's shooting, was his virtual obsession for rereading the script, studying every detail and still thinking of what he would do if he were directing it. There was always a director inside of Kirk Douglas, but it would take several more years before it would get out.

Even the producer in Kirk Douglas was somewhat subdued now, as he allowed himself to be hired by other producers. He had been paid a fee of 400,000 dollars to do *In Harm's Way*, and it hadn't hurt. It must have been reassuring for him to know that he was still a viable commodity. In fact, such was his status that even those with a grudge against him were sometimes willing to forget the past. Such a man was Anthony Mann.

Mann had not suffered at all after being fired by Douglas early in the shooting stages of *Spartacus*. He had found immediate work in filming the colourful remake of *Cimarron*, a large-scale western which was only diminished when compared to the original version. Then he had gone on to direct an equally successful and far superior historical epic to *Spartacus—El Cid*. This in turn led to an even bigger though less successful spectacle, *The Fall Of The Roman Empire*. Through such films Mann had established himself as one of the most important directors of the Sixties and a specialist in lavish screen entertainment. Tragically, he died in 1967 midway through production on *A Dandy In Aspic*. But before his untimely death he got to work with Kirk finally in 1965 on another war picture, *The Heroes Of Telemark*.

It told the true story of two raids made by the Norwegian resistance against the German atomic programme which succeeded in foiling the German efforts to create the atomic bomb. Douglas played a scientist who leads these attacks. Co-starring was Richard Harris as a Norwegian underground leader.

Kirk told me that he made *The Heroes Of Telemark* as a favour to Mann because he had fired the director five years earlier. Mann certainly wanted Douglas for his film in the hope Kirk would provide some box office assurance. Richard Harris at that time was a fast-rising star, but one with as bad a reputation as Kirk when it came to on-set feuds. He had rowed with

Marlon Brando on the set of *Mutiny On The Bounty* to the point where Brando refused to appear in any more scenes with him, and he had fallen foul of Charlton Heston when they made *Major Dundee* just prior to *Heroes Of Telemark*. Now he wasn't getting along at all well with Kirk Douglas.

Perhaps the problem with Harris was that he was too much like Kirk Douglas. 'I ring up a director at two o'clock in the morning to discuss a scene,' Harris says. 'I turn up on the set with twenty pages of notes. I say, this is true cooperation.' Directors may not always think so. And with Kirk Douglas working to the same kind of formula, it was inevitable that when working on the same picture, the two stars would clash.

It was a tough film to make. Part of it was shot in England, but for two months the whole company worked in sub-zero temperatures in Norway. At least they enjoyed a white Christmas that year of 1964. For most of the unit, making *The Heroes Of Telemark* was a cold and miserable experience, but for Kirk it provided the kind of authenticity he always sought. It helped him to act being cold if he really was cold. But sometimes just feeling cold wasn't enough to satisfy Anthony Mann. 'When Kirk Douglas or Richard Harris didn't look cold enough,' Mann once said, 'I'd go up to them with a handful of powdery snow and blow it in their faces, putting an icy frosting on their eyebrows.'

Despite the discomforts, Douglas enjoyed making *The Heroes Of Telemark*. Because it was a true story and comparatively recent, there was an abundance of research material for him to study, not least of which was the book *Skis Against The Atom* by Knut Haukelid, on which the film was based.

He was delighted to have on the set Lieutenant Colonel Haukfield, who was the one who actually led the attack on the heavy water factory and, later, the ferry which carried the necessary heavy water. Kirk spent hours with him, talking about the raids that were so vital in turning the war in the allies' favour.

There was also fun to be had. Kirk loved playing snowballs and would do so at every opportunity, much to the annoyance of Anthony Mann, who attempted to keep diligent guard against the snow being spoiled. Kirk also learned how to ski, as did the rest of the cast, which included Ulla Jacobson and

Michael Redgrave. Kirk was delighted to have a Norwegian skiing champion coach him. In fact, Kirk, who had filmed *The Vikings* in Norway, was impressed with the Norwegian cooperation on this production. He said that it was of a kind he had seldom encountered anywhere.

The finished film was an exciting, tension-filled wartime adventure. But it came too late in the cycle of large-scale war films which was produced in the early Sixties. *The Great Escape* had by and large changed the attitude of the audience regarding war films. They expected not just stacks of action, but plenty of comedy too. *The Heroes Of Telemark* had little humour to offer, although it did prove popular among schoolboys and always did better when playing matinees during school holidays.

Immediately following *The Heroes Of Telemark* Kirk went off to Israel to star in another epic war film, *Cast A Giant Shadow*. This time it was not set during the Second World War, but told the true story of the conflict between the Israelis and the Arabs in 1947. Kirk portrayed another true-life character, Colonel David 'Mickey' Marcus, an American soldier who was persuaded by the Israeli government to organize and command an army to repel the Arabs following the British withdrawal from Palestine.

Melville Shavelson wrote, produced and directed this giant picture and, it seemed, forever after regretted it. In the hope of ensuring his film had as much box office appeal as possible, he hired a handful of top stars to make cameo appearances. These were John Wayne, Yul Brynner and Frank Sinatra. He also tried to popularize the movie by adding some fictional romantic angles. Lovely Viennese actress Senta Berger was given the fictitious role of a freedom-fighter for Douglas to fall in love with.

These were all elements for which Shavelson was severely criticized. Yet he had done nothing that other film makers didn't do. History on the screen is seldom as it actually was, and as for the three cameos, it was nothing compared to other more critically acclaimed films like *The Longest Day*, *The Towering Inferno* and *The Battle Of Midway*, all of which really featured nothing but cameos.

Shavelson also encountered numberless problems in the

making of this film, not the least of which was hiring Kirk Douglas as his star. As soon as Kirk arrived on the set fresh from sabotaging German targets in Norway, he was ready to do battle again. Shavelson was quite astounded by Douglas, who it turned out knew the whole screenplay as well as Shavelson. Most actors, the director knew, only ever read their own parts thoroughly and so often they had only the shallowest of understanding regarding the film's concept. But Kirk Douglas had not only read and remembered everybody else's lines of dialogue, he had also read the director's scripted instructions.

Before Mel knew where he was, Kirk was meeting with him to discuss every aspect of the screenplay. Kirk, his director discovered, argued every point in every scene which he didn't understand, and didn't let up until he either saw it the director's way or did his best to change it to suit his own concept. The problem was, Kirk was dealing here with the man who was not only directing and producing this mammoth project, but had also written the screenplay and had his own conception of what his own film was all about. To Mel's relief, he found Kirk to be not only intelligent but also a man of logic. He was prepared to listen to the director's point of view, and Mel always knew he had to give logical arguments. In this manner Mel and Kirk were able to work together, but it was tough on Shavelson, probably as tough as it had ever been for him in a working relationship with any actor.

There were also problems in making such a large-scale film in Israel, a country where they were not yet used to making such epics, which is surprising since most epics have been about Israel. Yet never before had a movie of such size been shot there. And with so many thousands of extras and so much hardware enlisted for the film, there were bound to be delays, accidents, lost tempers and added expense to an already expensive movie.

All of this, coupled with the film's failure at the box office, prompted Mel Shavelson to write a now classic book, *How To Make A Jewish Movie*. It tells in the most humorous terms of the trials and tribulations of making *Cast A Giant Shadow*. Yet I suspect that Kirk doesn't share Mel's point of view that the film was a farce either in the making or in the finished result. Kirk told me:

107

Well, Mel wanted to write a book, and you can't write a book and say there were no problems. I mean, drama is built on problems and contrasts. I think all in all, Mel Shavelson did have problems in the making of *Cast A Giant Shadow*. And I think one of the problems he had, and I know because I'm guilty of this very often, is wearing too many hats. He was the writer and the director and the producer. You need somebody else to bounce things off of.

But I think all in all the biggest problem to me as I look back on *Cast A Giant Shadow* was top heavy actors that were unnecessary. Too many stars which we really didn't need. It was nice to play with Sinatra and Brynner and Wayne, but sometimes I think these cameos are a cheat. They asked me to do one in *Midway*. I resent it. I think it's like cheating the public. In certain situations, they have cameos just to get a lot of big names on the marquee.

There were certainly other problems which kept setting the film schedule back while forcing the budget up. The cast and crew spent some time in Italy filming in a village near Rome. These scenes featured Kirk Douglas and John Wayne and were part of a series of flashbacks to the Second World War. After all the necessary footage was in the can, a reel of film worth about 70,000 dollars was stolen. As if that wasn't bad enough, the shooting of that sequence had already been held up and made all the more expensive when filming had to be postponed after John Wayne was injured. He was shooting a scene with Kirk Douglas in which the two are fired upon by a German sniper. The two hit the dirt. But as Wayne went down, he slipped a disc and had to be hospitalized.

It wasn't all doom and despondency, though, for Kirk. He had all four of his sons with him on location. Both Joel and Michael were working as production assistants, giving both boys good grounding for their future careers as film producers. Michael had also served as assistant director on *The Heroes Of Telemark*. Kirk's younger sons, Eric and Peter, seven and nine years old, were having a whale of a time just being around dad and seeing a film being made. The problem was, Kirk was unwittingly encouraging his sons to look towards careers in films, while consciously he had always done his best to dissuade them from going into the business. It was just that his enthusiasm for fatherhood ensured that he spent as much time with his kids as was possible. He had learned two valuable lessons regarding parenthood. He had learned how not to be a parent from his own father. And he had also learned that there were an awful lot of 'orphans' in Hollywood whose parents were always off and filming, finding little time to be a complete family. But in sowing the seeds of family unity, Kirk was also sowing the seeds of ambition in his sons which he would rather have avoided. And yet, as shall be seen, he was never any the less proud of them for what they did eventually achieve.

Whatever the problems encountered in the making of this film, Kirk always took his part in its making seriously and conscientiously, just like 'Mickey' Marcus did in real life.

It was a film which also gave him the opportunity to grow a little closer to John Wayne who, in fact, suggested that Kirk play the part of Marcus. 'I like John Wayne,' Kirk once told me before Wayne's death. 'We don't see eye to eye on a lot of things, but I've got tremendous respect for him. To me, Wayne is a real professional. He's a much better actor than he's often given credit for.

'The reason I made *Cast A Giant Shadow* was because Wayne called me and said, "Listen, I've got this script which I think is perfect for you. If you play it, I'll play the small part of the General." And he did. Wayne is an amazing institution. They don't make that kind any more.'

After *Cast A Giant Shadow*, Kirk broke his own rule about making cameo appearances by agreeing to do one scene in yet another long, expensive epic about the Second World War, *Is Paris Burning?* It was a French-American co-production, produced by Ray Stark for the American contingent and Paul Graetz on behalf of the French. Frenchman Rene Clement directed. Kirk's role was that of General Patton. It was not the most demanding part. All he really had to do was be himself in uniform and speak some lines of dialogue. He turned up among numerous other big star names from both America and France, including Jean-Paul Belmondo, Charles Boyer, Leslie Caron, George Chakiris, Alain Delon, Glenn Ford, Anthony Perkins, Robert Stack and Orson Welles.

When I had the chance to challenge Kirk about his participation in this film considering his remarks about cameos, he told me, 'Ray Stark who's a friend of mine asked me to do it and I did it. It took just one day. It was a *long* day!'

A long day indeed. The director Rene Clement was under tremendous pressure to complete Kirk's scene in such a short time not just because Kirk was only available for the day but also because Clement had an absolutely gruelling schedule to stick to. Such a scene would normally have taken maybe two or three days to shoot comfortably.

Kirk should have been well pleased not to be any deeper involved with the film. Making the film was much like a military operation, with Clement dividing his crew into units to film different sequences simultaneously in the actual streets of Paris, all of which had to be blocked off from the public at times agreed with the French authorities.

With that little bit of film work completed, Kirk's presence in Europe was taken advantage of by the US Information Agency, who had him tour several countries in the latter part of 1965 as their official goodwill ambassador. After that he and Anne were off doing the same in the Middle East. Kirk performed on behalf of the State Department with little if any publicity. One suspects that he wouldn't have wanted his 'difficult' image tarnished by the revelation that he was abroad spreading goodwill instead of ill-feeling. But it was a job he undertook with much pride and soberness. He knew that as an actor he had some degree of influence, and he was glad to be able to use it for his country's cause. He says:

> Artists have a universal language the world over, like athletes and musicians. They are good ambassadors for their countries because they transcend political lines. They become the cement that ties people together in the world. I am also very much in favour of co-productions because this opens up a dialogue with another country and can be more important than the making of a film.

This line of work continued in 1966 when President Lyndon B. Johnson sent Kirk behind the Iron Curtain. Again Anne went with him, and together they visited Poland, Romania,

Bulgaria, Hungary, Czechoslovakia and Yugoslavia. It was his first real view of communism. He was not impressed by it.

Tito of Yugoslavia was an ardent movie fan. Kirk had successfully negotiated a private interview with Tito, who told Kirk that he watched at least one film almost every night. He was also very knowledgeable on Kirk's films.

Kirk asked him why he loved movies so much.

'Because I find them relaxing,' replied Tito. 'If I watch you in *The Vikings*, I can forget all my problems for a little while.'

After the meeting, Kirk was approached by the British Ambassador. He explained to Kirk that he'd been trying unsuccessfully for days to get to see Tito, and here was an American movie star who virtually just walks in.

'Why did Tito see you so eagerly?' asked the Ambassador.

'Mr Ambassador,' said Kirk, 'how many movies have *you* made?'

ELEVEN/ The Way West and Back Again

Kirk has always been aware that many directors tend to react like a cat stepping away from wet cement whenever they learn that Kirk Douglas is to be their leading star. He doesn't believe that he is entirely at fault, but he does concede that his manner and attitude can affect his relationship with the people he works with. He says:

> I'm outspoken, perhaps too much so. But I imagine it's my way of saying things rather than what I say that makes people mad. I've always insisted on voicing my suggestions with directors. The good ones have never objected. I find the secure person will listen to you and be open, but the insecure man is fighting for his own dominance, and he's afraid that accepting another person's point of view will weaken his.

There is no doubt that there have been movie directors with whom Kirk has worked who did resent his attempts to inject his own ideas. And it is this part of his considerable reputation which was going before him in the Sixties. Even seasoned directors faced the prospect of working with Kirk Douglas with trepidation. Andrew V. McLaglen was a case in point when he came to direct Kirk in yet another ambitious movie, though this time a western, *The Way West*.

McLaglen looks back on the experience and laughs about it now. He told me:

> It's a funny thing but I remember gritting myself for Kirk for about two months because of his reputation for being difficult. I was wondering what kind of problems I'd come up against, having heard how impossible he was to be directed.
>
> We also had Robert Mitchum and Richard Widmark in the cast, but I knew that they were easy to work with and I'd have no problems with them. In fact, usually the egos I come up against are from the supporting players.
>
> But funnily enough, when I met Kirk and started to work with him, I sort of felt like I'd known him in some other life. It was a funny feeling to meet someone like that and feel that way. And I found out he wasn't difficult at all. Not with me anyway. We got on famously.

That Kirk should have come to star in *The Way West* is quite ironic. The part he played, that of an ambitious, fanatical senator who organizes the Oregon Liberty Company and inspires emigrants to follow him across the wilderness to paradise, was one which was originally to be played by Burt Lancaster. When Lancaster was in partnership with James Hill and Harold Hecht, they purchased the film rights to the Pulitzer Prize-winning novel, *The Way West* by A. B. Guthrie. The intention was that they produce the film for Burt to star in. However, at the time, around 1960, they couldn't find the considerable financial backing to get the project off the ground.

Harold Hecht eventually went into producing films on his own, and in 1965 he managed to interest Charlton Heston in playing the part of Tadlock, which strengthened his position considerably in getting United Artists to put up the money. Hecht already had Andy McLaglen lined up to direct, and with Heston almost committed to the film, he then succeeded in the early part of 1966 of casting Widmark in the role of the reluctant scout and Mitchum as the father of a family heading for Oregon. However, Widmark and Mitchum got together and decided they would rather play each other's part, and so they swapped roles.

Meanwhile, Heston was having misgivings about the project. He was initially unimpressed with McLaglen's work, and eventually he pulled out of the project. Now Hecht wanted Kirk Douglas whom McLaglen had misgivings about, but as it happened, it all worked out fine. But the final irony is that Kirk ended up playing the part his terrible twin, Burt Lancaster, was supposed to have played at the outset.

Kirk enjoyed playing Tadlock, a difficult part because he had to portray a persuasive, inspiring man yet one whose ambition and obsession have driven his wife to suicide. As the trek across the plains progresses, his fanaticism becomes evident to the point where he is toppled from his powerful position by Widmark. 'You hate Tadlock, and you love him,' was how Kirk described the complex character. 'You're never indifferent to him.'

To assist him in his portrayal, Kirk read up on the life of Thomas Hart Benson, an expansionist senator whose lifelong ambition was to civilize the far west and make it all American. This too is the dream of Tadlock.

Throughout his career Kirk had experienced some tough locations. But on *The Way West* he and the rest of the cast and crew had something of a unique experience. For three months they retraced the steps of the early pioneers along the Oregon Trail, 2,000 miles from Montana to Oregon. In 1843 it had cost about 140 dollars to take a covered wagon train over the laborious trail. In 1966 it cost Hecht about 26,000 dollars a day to roll his covered wagons over the same stretch.

Douglas, Widmark, Mitchum and the rest of the cast found themselves experiencing something of what it was really like to make the pioneer journey. Kirk was always eager to do everything his own character was expected to do within the realms of safety. When they filmed the river-crossing sequence on the Willamette River, Kirk and the other actors took the plunge. They also braved the dizzying heights of Mount Bachelor, 7,700 feet high and on which director McLaglen suffered 'mountain fever' and had to be rescued by stuntmen when he froze with panic while hanging on to the side of the mountain with a sheer drop below him.

It was as much an endurance test for all concerned as it was a matter of telling a story on film. Kirk found it a revelation just to discover the unspoiled land that still looked exactly as it had done 124 years earlier. All of this is beautifully captured on film by cinematographer William H. Clothier. But overall the film failed to capture the spirit of the book. McLaglen blames the studio for re-editing the picture and turning it into a handsome-looking but run-of-the-mill western about wagon trains.

Kirk as usual dominated the film. He was fifty now, but he certainly didn't lack energy or sheer nerve. In one sequence he leads his wagon train in a rip-roaring race to the river, trying to beat a rival train. Kirk hardly flinched at the prospect of riding a horse at full gallop while all about him wagons thundered along. There was no back projection with Kirk riding a fake horse. He was really out there. That Kirk should have been performing physically demanding stunts at the age of fifty should not be too surprising, since even now, some seventeen years later, he is still able to perform feats of derring-do with amazing dexterity. 'Fitness is important,' he says. 'Vitality and energy are tied to acting. I often stand when others sit, I walk when others run. Moviemaking is a draining experience, and without health you just can't function, not in art and not in life. I approach a new picture like an athlete.'

He must have put in some strict training for his next picture, made in 1967. It was another western, *The War Wagon*, but totally unlike *The Way West*. This picture was for fun, and it teamed him again with John Wayne. Wayne was then sixty and beginning to get paunchy following his first bout with cancer. But Kirk was still lean and athletic. Among the feats he had to perform were vaulting on to a horse, leaping over railings, and swinging on a hanging saloon candle-holder in the manner of Errol Flynn.

Burt Kennedy directed this lively horse opera, injecting humour into the action. In one scene he wanted to feature a shot showing Kirk's bare behind. The censor cut it out. In another scene Wayne and Douglas are put to the test when two gunmen face them down. Our two heroes bet on who will drop their man first. After the brief showdown in which the two heavies are killed, Douglas triumphantly claims, 'Mine hit the ground first.' 'Mine was taller,' retorts Wayne.

This level of fun on screen was indicative of the fun had by all off screen. Kirk continued to enjoy working with Wayne, but, as before, he and the Duke never really got to socialize much after shooting hours. Nevertheless, Kirk's respect for Wayne was always strong, and has remained so five years after the Duke died.

'He was extremely professional,' says Kirk. 'He'd be the first on the set. He'd be down there looking over the special effects and asking what kind of dynamite they were using. He was interested in every aspect of film making.

'I think Wayne was an artist and a terrific human being. He handled his adversaries with dignity. He was unique.'

The story of *The War Wagon* centred around an armoured stagecoach complete with Gatling gun owned and operated by a crooked mine-owner, played by Bruce Cabot. Wayne plays a man out to wreak vengeance on Cabot who had framed Wayne and sent him to jail. Douglas played a gunman hired by Cabot to kill Wayne, but seeing the opportunity to rob the war wagon which is due to carry thousands of dollars worth of gold bullion, he joins up with Wayne. An odd assortment of characters joins their small gang, including Howard Keel as an hilarious Indian, Robert Walker as a drunk explosives expert, and mean old Keenan Wynn.

Also in the cast in a small supporting part was a then unknown Bruce Dern. Dern was making quite a good living playing killers and freaks in westerns and motorcycle pictures. It was to be some years before he would start getting some really good film roles. But even at this early time, Kirk, ever the producer as well as actor, was watching him. He saw tremendous potential in Dern. One day he said to Dern, 'One day I'm going to find a really good film role for you in one of my pictures.' Dern thought he was just kidding, but it was a promise Kirk would keep.

The War Wagon was the eleventh western Kirk had appeared in. He always enjoyed the opportunity to put on cowboy hats and boots and to twirl guns. He said:

> No actor I know would turn down a good role in a western. Practically all of my colleagues, from comedians to the most sophisticated types, are on the lookout for a cowboy flick. They may claim that they want to do one as a

change of pace, or a chance to show their versatility. The truth is that they are just as much drawn to the gun-toting hero as the child who wants his first present to be a holster and cowboy hat.

Psychologists try to explain this perpetual enthusiasm for westerns in terms of symbolism. They find in the gun, the horse, the ten-gallon hat and the wide-open spaces symbols which are unconsciously significant to an audience. The same story told in different terms wouldn't have the same impact. So say the psychologists, and I suppose their guess is as good as anyone else's.

What, then, is the secret of the western's appeal? Is it plot? I doubt it. The plot of most westerns is simple. And how many different plots could possibly be contrived for the thousands of westerns that have been filmed over the years?

I think the essential appeal lies in the character of the cowboy himself. He is the cult idol around whom this whole form of worship revolves.

This was, of course, at a time when westerns were still extremely popular and Wayne was king of the cowboys. Today few westerns are made. Yet Kirk still makes westerns, as shall be seen.

During the late Sixties westerns were still among the most popular pictures around. But in 1968 Clint Eastwood, who had made his name in spaghetti westerns, went from the West to the East to make a New York-based cop film, *Coogan's Bluff*. It was slick, violent and introduced a new breed of tough cop. Universal, who made it, suddenly put much of their efforts into turning out similar crime stories, all following the same basic formula—tough policeman in New York who gets his man, any way he can. Many stars, some of them mostly famous for appearing in westerns, made the on-screen migration back to the East Coast to make similar films such as *Madigan* with Richard Widmark, and *PJ* with George Peppard.

Kirk's contribution was *A Lovely Way To Die*. He played a cop with the unlikely name of Jim Schuyler with a reputation for being excessive in his tough treatment of criminals. When he is scolded for his methods, he resigns and takes a job as a body-

117

guard to lovely Sylvia Koscina. Inevitably he falls in love with the body he's guarding. The trouble is, she's on a charge of murder, and he sets out to solve the case and prove her innocent.

The drama that unfolded on the screen, however, was superficial and meagre compared to the one that was taking place in Kirk's family life.

TWELVE/
/Son of Spartacus

For more than twenty years Kirk had devoted his life to trying to become the father he never had.

Even following his divorce from Diana, he remained close to his sons Michael and Joel. Being his first, Michael had always been the apple of his father's eye, though this did nothing to detract from the love and attention Kirk showed to Joel and his other sons Peter and Eric. With his money he was able to buy them the things that they needed, and that sometimes meant the things that they wanted. They lacked for nothing, even though Michael and Joel lived most of the time with their mother. But Kirk also knew from his own personal experience that the very most he could do for his children was to see that they gain an education and find some vocation in life:

I only watch, as any father should, to see whether they select the métier which is best for them.

And with all of them I've insisted on education. The basis of education is to enable you to think for yourself. All that I ask of my sons is that they function. I would never permit them to vegetate, as too many of their generation do. I don't care what they *do*, as long as they are doing something.

It's a precious thing to retain the individuality of a child, and try to help that child develop his own personality and way of life so that he doesn't have the shadow of his parents smothering him.

I insist on education.

And an education is what they got. Michael, for instance, went to schools in New York, Connecticut and California. He became a graduate from the University of California. He was a bright, intelligent young man and Kirk had great hopes for him. But he always hoped Michael would find something else to do other than be a film maker.

But it was never that easy for Michael. His father had verbally discouraged him from becoming an actor, yet he allowed his son to work behind the scenes on some of his films, though that was more in the way of giving his children the opportunity of being close to dad when he was working without getting lazy. Despite Kirk's desire that he never overshadow his sons, it was in fact something that was inevitable. Kirk Douglas was one of the world's best-known personalities. By virtue of his blood, Michael Douglas was in the limelight too. He was always 'the son of Kirk Douglas'. He even looked like dad, except that he didn't have a .dimple on his chin. Michael seemed to have no identity of his own. He was carrying his father's identity around through no fault of his own or Kirk's. He felt he had to make a life for himself which would be as different from his father's as possible.

It was the late Sixties. It was the time of flower power. Long hair. Ban the bomb. Drugs. Love-ins. Communes. American soldiers were dying in Vietnam. A whole generation was in open rebellion. They cried, 'Make love, not war.' They did their own thing. Michael did his. He grew his hair long, dropped out of the life he was in, and fell away from Kirk. Dad didn't seem to understand. How could he? He was so much older. An entirely different generation. Determined to be free of his father's shadow, Michael fled to a hippy commune. After all, how could dad understand how he felt?

Dad understood a great deal.

Current trends don't surprise me at all. The changes that are taking place are ones which the youth of today have perpetuated.

Various views of Kirk Douglas, reading clockwise: the second-in-command to John Wayne's naval captain in In Harm's Way *(1965), the middle-aged mafioso in* The Brotherhood *(1969), the ambitious fanatic who inspired people to follow him across the wilderness to paradise in* The Way West *(1967), and the corrupt US marshal in* Posse *(1975).*

'There are no roles for fat leading men,' said Kirk Douglas — at the time
his leading lady was Farah Fawcett in Saturn 3 (1979). He remained lean,
fit and active to take two parts in the Australian film The Man From
Snowy River (1981) — he played twin brothers. Jack Thompson was a
rider who shared his adventures.

Kirk and a stuntman on the set of Spartacus — *he insisted in taking part in the film's thrilling gladiatorial contest himself (it took twelve days to film the sequence, which lasts just seven minutes on the screen). Fortunately, he survived unscathed to enjoy his wife and their two sons, Eric and Peter.*

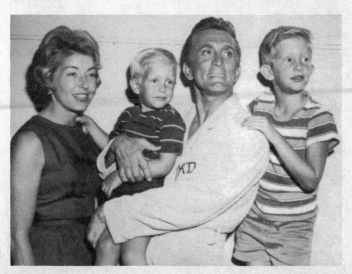

As the bewildered aide of an ambitious general (played by Burt Lancaster) in Seven Days in May *(1964) — a military drama about an attempt to depose a pacifist President.*

Kirk Douglas enjoyed disguises — and playing a wide range of characters. In 1954 he appeared in 20,000 Leagues Under the Sea *as harpoonist Ned Lands (seen here with James Mason, Peter Lorre and Paul Lucas), and as Homer's hero in* Ulysses. *Three years later he was a major-general in* Top Secret Affair *(1957).*

In Lust for Life *(1956), the biography of Vincent Van Gogh, Kirk achieved a startling resemblance to the artist by growing a beard and dying his hair. He also learned to paint, taking lessons from a French artist: 'I am not one of art's great immortals, but at least I can catch a crow in flight,' he claims.*

For his role as an unscrupulous fighter in Champion *(1949), Kirk took boxing lessons — and a gamble in accepting the modest fee offered him by the then scarcely-known Stanley Kramer. It paid off; he was nominated for a Best Actor Academy Award, and the film was a knock-out at the box office.*

In The Bad and the Beautiful *(1952), Douglas played a ruthless movie producer who rose to the top in Hollywood — again, he was nominated as Best Actor. Here he is with leading lady Lana Turner, and on the set.*

Ten years later he played an actor turned director in another movie about movies, Two Weeks in Another Town, *which used footage from* The Bad and the Beautiful *to illustrate the character's former career!*

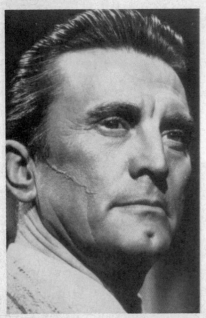

There's always danger in revolution, but I think it's good that they are questioning the establishment. I only hope they are fully aware that the pendulum can swing the other way. It's much easier to criticize a situation than to correct it.

But I think it's healthy that our children have questioned the moral values of the adult world, although I don't see much difference now from the days when my generation was considered rebellious.

As an interested onlooker I think it boils down to a good imagination on the child's part and a good memory on the parent's. A child can only imagine what it must be like to be a parent, and a parent ought to remember what it's like to be a child.

There was no way Kirk could criticize what Michael was doing. He had himself shunned the system to get where he was, and Michael was trying to do the same to get to wherever he was going. It was such a character that was portrayed by Kirk in *Lonely Are The Brave*. The lonely cowboy had only wanted to live on his own terms. So did Michael.

But Kirk was concerned about the way in which Michael was going about it. He felt he had to intervene in some way. So he went to visit his son at the commune. Kirk was shocked by what he saw. The house where Michael lived was full of hippies, high on marijuana or whatever, and the place was filthy. There was no inside toilet: that was in an outhouse. Kirk had gone there with the intention, not of bringing his son home forcibly, since Michael was now in his twenties, but simply to be his son's friend. He had agreed to stay the night. He wondered what he had got himself into. That night Kirk slept on Michael's bed which sagged uncomfortably in the middle. Michael was happy enough to sleep on the floor. Kirk hated the experience. He told Michael, 'Listen son, my whole life I've been trying to get out of places like this.'

At least Kirk had proven that he cared, and it struck a responsive chord in Michael. But what Michael really wanted was to be an actor, and not to be the son of Kirk Douglas. He wanted only to be Michael Douglas, who made it on his own. He had indeed been studying acting for several years and had not sought help from Kirk. At the University of California he

121

had been named the best actor of 1967. But always the shadow of Kirk Douglas hung over him.

In 1969 Michael landed a big break when he was in New York in a television production called *The Experiment*. Straight after that he returned to Hollywood to audition for a film called *Hail, Hero*, a story about the problems confronting the youth of that time. He was just one of many others who were also tested for the part, and he felt sceptical about his chances. But the film's producer, Harold D. Cohen, was so impressed with Michael that he offered him the role.

A few weeks after that, *The Experiment* was aired, and Michael received a great deal of praise from the critics. Suddenly other Hollywood producers were eager to have Michael Douglas signed to them, but Cohen had got there first and Michael was all set to do his first film, *Hail, Hero*.

He was now off and running as an actor. The following year he made *Adam At 6 AM*, followed by Disney's *Napoleon And Samantha*, which featured an infant Jodie Foster, and *Summertree* in which he co-starred with Brenda Vaccaro. On that film he and Brenda fell in love and began a long live-in relationship. Kirk was able to breathe a sigh of relief. Michael wasn't married, but he had at last began to settle down and he was making a go of it as an actor. The only problem was, Michael was still known as the son of Kirk. But that would change in time.

THIRTEEN/
/New Directions

While Michael was having to sort out his life, Kirk was busy trying to reorganize his own career. He had not produced a film of his own since *Seven Days In May*. Since then he had enjoyed making films for other people but had been frustrated at the limitations imposed on him when what he really wanted to do was get in there and make a film on his own terms.

It was time, he felt, to make the kind of picture he envisioned, and he chose to make a daring film about the Mafia. It was daring because prior to *The Godfather* the Mafia had never been considered suitable as a subject for motion picture entertainment. If a film ever did feature the Mafia, the organization was never mentioned by name.

If anyone had the guts to film a story about the Mafia, it was Kirk Douglas. He had writer Lewis John Carlino fashion an original screenplay called *The Brotherhood*, and hired noted director Martin Ritt to helm the filming. Kirk then assembled a first-rate cast with Alex Cord, Irene Papas, Luther Adler, Susan Strasberg and a host of fine character actors to portray the older men of the syndicate. One of these was eighty-two-year-old Eduardo Ciannelli, who died just a couple of years after completing *The Brotherhood*.

As with all Kirk Douglas productions, the technical aspects of the film were first-class. If ever Kirk could be faulted as a producer, it was that sometimes the content of his films didn't always match the production values, as with *The Last Sunset* and even *The Vikings*. He always made handsome-looking movies, but they were not always matched by superior screenplays and plots.

The problem with *The Brotherhood* wasn't in the screenplay which was of excellent quality, nor in the direction which was frighteningly stark, nor in the performances all of which deserved high merit. The big challenge with *The Brotherhood* was in its concept. Kirk expects the audience to take sides when presenting the old-style Mafia brotherhood in conflict with the new generation of gangsters. However, the moral implications aside, Kirk does deliver a fascinating glimpse into the underworld where crime is just a way of life.

In the film he plays a middle-aged gangster, born and bred within the Mafia and dedicated to its dubious cause. He is proud of his criminal activities and is loyal to the old system. His brother, Alex Cord, however, is bent on tackling new businesses of the Space Age. After brutally murdering a gangster who betrayed and caused the massacre of forty Mafia leaders, Douglas flees to Sicily with his wife and daughter and retires. Finally the younger brother turns up and Douglas knows that his rival syndicate leaders have sent Cord to kill him. He makes it easy for Cord, taking him to a quiet grove, handing him a rifle and then kissing his brother full on the lips—the Mafia kiss of death. It's an open invitation which Cord is obliged to accept or face having his own family slaughtered.

Because of the film's moral problems and not because of any lack of quality, *The Brotherhood* did not gell with audiences. Kirk's hunch that audiences could identify with the characters because they were simply family men involved in big business didn't pay off. The film was a flop on its release in 1969.

Kirk now felt he had to allow his instincts to go with a film maker whose reputation was legendary—Elia Kazan. In many ways this offered safety, but more important to Kirk, the film Kazan was offering him, *The Arrangement*, was one which Kirk could see the potential in and loved. Kazan had written the screenplay from his own book which he confesses is somewhat autobiographical. The novel had been a best-seller, and everything indicated that the film would be a smash.

It was the story of a brilliant advertising executive, Eddie, who has wealth and a wife. He also has a sultry mistress. But he feels that there is something lacking in his life, and so he tries to kill himself. He runs his car into a truck but survives the accident. He recovers after a long convalescence but is mentally distraught. Much of the story features him fantasizing about his mistress and remembering his tyrannical father and over-powering mother, and after failing to make it back into business, decides to rescue his ailing father from the clutches of the doctors. He then takes up residence with his mistress who has another lover who shoots Eddie. But he still survives and insists they put him in an institution. Finally the wife and the mistress make a truce in an effort to get their man back on the tracks again.

The main role had been offered to Marlon Brando, with whom Kazan had worked in *On The Waterfront*. But after Brando dropped out of the film Warner Bros, who were backing the picture, suggested to Kazan that he approach Kirk Douglas. Kazan was appalled at the suggestion. He didn't believe Douglas had the depth or personality to carry this role off, and in desperation for a more hopeful solution, he tried to interest Charlton Heston. Heston was tempted at the prospect of working with the great Kazan, but was unimpressed with both the book and the script.

So reluctantly Kazan offered the film to Douglas. Kirk read the script and found he had much in common with the lead character, Eddie:

> I knew exactly what Kazan had in mind about his hero Eddie. Here was a middle-aged man who one day looked in the mirror and didn't like what he saw—the phoney Madison Avenue image of the affluent advertising executive. So he tried to turn hippy—twenty years too late and with disastrous results.
>
> A lot of my playing of Eddie was autobiographical. I'm not discontented with my own life. I've done well, but I know that kind of man and how he got that way, and I can understand why the younger generation look at us with disdain.

Despite his initial misgivings concerning Douglas, Kazan discovered that he not only liked working with Douglas, but that he also found that Kirk was a much better actor than he'd given him credit for. In fact, Kazan was delighted with the goods that Kirk delivered in his performance. It was a role which Kirk took hold of in both hands and totally immersed himself in.

Kazan had hand-picked an excellent cast to perform with Kirk, including Deborah Kerr as the wife, Faye Dunaway as the mistress, and Richard Boone as the sick father.

It being the so-called permissive age, Kazan littered the film with a number of rather candid sex scenes and plenty of strong language. But none of this was enough to make the film a commercial success.

Kirk had been down before. He knew he would be back, and when Joseph L. Mankiewicz offered him an off-beat western, *There Was A Crooked Man*, Kirk accepted, remembering the glories of *A Letter To Three Wives* in 1949. The film was set in a territorial prison during the 1880s. Warner Bros spent 300,000 dollars alone in constructing the impressive and realistic prison in the high desert country of the Joshua Tree National Monument.

The film seemed to be little more than a story of escape. But as one gets into the film, it becomes clear that here is a cynical view of westerns and the traditional heroes. Douglas is an outlaw who, like the protagonists of many spaghetti westerns, takes delight in killing his own men. After the long-awaited escape towards the end of the picture, Douglas murders the men who helped him. He rides to a rattlesnake pit where some loot of his has been long hidden, and he gets fatally bitten by a snake. Then along comes Henry Fonda, who all the way through the film has portrayed a loyal sheriff, and steals the money for himself and heads for Mexico.

Before the film had been cast, Mankiewicz and his screenwriters David Newman and Robert Benton had met with the entire production team to propose two suitable candidates for the leading roles. Various teams were suggested, including John Wayne and Warren Beatty. But it was the pairing of Kirk Douglas and Henry Fonda which won.

The picture was made under circumstances that were not

exactly favourable. Mankiewicz discovered a great change in Douglas since they had last worked together twenty years before. Mankiewicz wanted certain nuances from Kirk but felt that Douglas now seemed to work in 'broad strokes' and was prepared only to take a limited amount of direction. He felt that Kirk knew what he wanted to do and what he was prepared to do, but anything beyond that was out of the question. Some of the blame must lie, though, with Mankiewicz, who admittedly didn't see this film to be a particularly important one. If he had done, he says, he would have fought harder with Kirk to get the responses he wanted.

It also seems that Fonda was not endeared to Kirk on the set of this film. It irritated Fonda to watch Kirk concerning himself with how to handle a prop cigar for instance rather than with the content of the scene.

Kirk, it seems, was just as disappointed with Mankiewicz. 'Elia Kazan is completely involved with you while Joe is detached, an observer,' he says. 'I didn't think he was comfortable with the elements of the western. He is best with mental rather than physical gymnastics.'

When it did come to the dialogue scenes, Mankiewicz was at his best. In one scene, Douglas tries to persuade Burgess Meredith to take part in the escape. Mankiewicz put the two actors through five takes, each one progressively superior. In fact, onlookers believing that take number three had looked like it couldn't be beaten asked why he continued to take further stabs at the scene. 'You have to know the actor,' said Mankiewicz. 'Some actors you have to keep pushing. But some just go downhill after the first take.' Mankiewicz knew that Douglas improved with each take.

One of the main faults with the film was that its cast was made up generally of veteran actors—a less kind observer might describe them as geriatrics. Douglas was now fifty-four, and Fonda was an amazing sixty-five. There was also Burgess Meredith aged sixty-two and Hume Cronyn, fifty-nine, who during production discovered he had optic cancer which needed an immediate operation. The only young actor in the film was Michael Blodgett. One of the first scenes he did was in a prison cell with Kirk Douglas, Meredith, Cronyn, John Randolph and Warren Oates. Mankiewicz told Blodgett, 'You'll be competing with a hundred-and-fifty years of scene-stealing experience in there.'

But the experience of all concerned wasn't enough to make the picture into a winner. Kirk was particularly disappointed and said, 'I thought the idea of the western was brilliant, but the exchange of ideas came too late in the third act when you need visuals, not talk. And the switch was equally brilliant, but it started too late in the picture.'

Determined that he could make a better yet more modest western, Kirk resurrected Bryna to produce *A Gunfight* in 1971. It turned out to be a remarkable little film; taut, tense and with the best surprise ending any western ever had. Kirk played to perfection a gunman who's getting sick of life and his reputation. He's lived a long life, but has now hung up his guns and settled down with a lovely wife, played by a brilliant actress from Broadway, Jane Alexander. He now works as a sort of tourist attraction in the saloon. When a famed gunslinger, played by Johnny Cash, rides into town, everyone suspects that there will be a showdown. But the two meet up in a cordial fashion over drinks at the bar. They have no intention of shooting it out until the town forces them into a confrontation when the townsfolk start placing bets on who will emerge the victor. Douglas is at the point in life where he could hardly care less, and persuades Cash that they could in fact stage a gunfight with paid admission. When the showdown comes in a bullfight arena, it is Douglas who is gunned down. Then, in a startling fantasy sequence—or is it?—Douglas's wife fancies that she sees Douglas emerge the winner.

With this film Kirk was in a way heading down the road with his western persona. He had played the traditional hero in *Gunfight At The OK Corral*, he'd played the last of a breed in *Lonely Are The Brave*, and he'd played the likeable rogue in *The War Wagon*. Now he was playing the gunman who'd grown tired—and in the role of his son was his own offspring, Eric.

In making *A Gunfight*, Kirk had gone into partnership with two young producers, Ronnie Lubin and Harold Jack Bloom, who had their own companies, Harvest and Thoroughbred. Talented director Lamont Johnson worked in close collaboration with Kirk, as any director on one of Douglas's films now certainly would have to do, and came up with a stylish western that could boast much originality as well as flair.

In setting up the production, Kirk had intended filming *A Gunfight* in Spain where innumerable westerns had been produced over the past several years, mainly by Italians, and where there was not only suitable financing to be found but also all the necessary sets, costumes and hardware. Film making in America had hit a slump and there were few films in production there. Most westerns were being made in Spain, then, and some in Mexico.

Kirk and his co-producers would have preferred to make their film at home rather than go all the way to Europe. By chance, word of the film reached a most unusual bunch of potential investors who decided to make a pitch to have Kirk make the film in New Mexico. They were the Jicarilia Apache Tribe of New Mexico. To Kirk's tremendous surprise, the Indians asked for a meeting with him and his partners. The Indians explained that they had heard a western was to be made and that they had money to pay for the production. Kirk and the other producers were agog as the Chief explained that his tribe of almost 2,000 had accumulated some considerable wealth from gas and oil lease incomes and deposits of uranium on their reservation lands.

Kirk felt it was only fair to explain to the Indians that there were no parts for the tribe since it wasn't about Indians at all. The Chief announced that they weren't looking for film roles. They just wanted to make an investment and figured a motion picture was a good bet. So they put up the whole of the two million dollars needed to make the film and it was made down in New Mexico, which was much more to everyone's liking.

The early Seventies was a bleak time for all in the American film industry. Cinema was in something of a crisis with astronomically rising costs. Fewer films than ever were being made, and very few of them were geared towards the veterans of Hollywood such as Kirk Douglas. It was the time of the new superstar. Personalities that appealed to youth were the ones in demand by the studios: Paul Newman, Robert Redford, Clint Eastwood, Barbra Streisand, Burt Reynolds and the like. The John Waynes, the James Stewarts, the Henry Fondas

129

and the Kirk Douglases were not enjoying the success they all had once known.

While the new breed of stars continued to earn millions making movies in Hollywood, some of the veterans made a wise move by accepting offers from European film makers. Henry Fonda was among these. Some like Wayne battled on in the States but to no avail. The Duke's films of the Seventies were generally poor.

Kirk Douglas was not prepared to stagnate in an early retirement. He knew the place to make his movies now was Europe. This really wasn't anything new to him. He had made a number of European films in the past. He'd met his wife while making one.

He was also intent on pursuing his course as a film producer. It was this move which had undoubtedly saved his career back in the Fifties. 'The impact of television brought enormous changes in the Hollywood studios, with fewer and fewer films being produced,' he explains. 'Many stars found themselves unemployed and I wasn't about to let it happen to me. Some of us formed our own companies. Burt Lancaster and John Wayne are among the best examples, and we made our own deals with the studios. It was a matter of survival.'

After the success of a number of his own productions in the late Fifties and early Sixties, Kirk again became highly employable. But now he and Hollywood were both in a rut, so Kirk began negotiating with foreign studios so that he could continue to act and produce.

He said:

> If we are to survive, we are going to have to be more international. The more we cross frontiers to make co-productions and multi-national financing the better it will be for the future of our industry.
>
> Film financing, like gold, is where you find it. Today we are interinvolved and interdependent, and the future is bound to see an increase in these trends.
>
> This is a healthy development. If you assemble a cast which has stars drawn from different countries, you have built-in appeal for those countries when it comes to selling and distributing. Also, it's good that technicians of differ-

ent countries work together. Film making is an international means of expression.

For his first in a series of European co-productions, Kirk acquired the screen rights of Jules Verne's pirate adventure, *The Light At The Edge Of The World*. Heading the American contingent was Kirk and his pal Yul Brynner. Samantha Eggar was from Britain, Jean Claude Drouot from France, and leading a vast array of Spanish actors was Fernando Rey. The director was England's Kevin Billington.

Kirk took his company to the Spanish coast, close to the French border, to film this peculiar pirate yarn. Unfortunately, the film suffered from Billington's limp direction, some erratic editing in its English version, and some rather graphic violence which took all the yo-ho-ho out of the pirate adventure.

Kirk freely admits, 'It wasn't a very good film.'

Neither is it a film which holds fond memories for Kirk in its making. In fact, it nearly killed him. Kirk, as usual, insisted on doing as many of the stunts as was possible, even though he had a stunt double on hand to do the really tricky stuff. For one scene Kirk had to climb over the roof of a building and leap on to a terrace. Kirk sized up the situation. It seemed easy enough and there were no obvious dangers, other than the fact that the building was perched on treacherous, dark, jagged rocks. Kirk knew he could do the stunt himself although he felt that he needed a platform built so that if he should topple when landing on the terrace, he would have the platform to break his fall. It was also suggested that some kind of fencing be put around the platform so he didn't fall off that. But Kirk didn't want to waste time. He said that his stunt double could stand on the platform, ready to catch him.

So Kirk did the leap from the roof. As he had anticipated, he wound up on the platform. The stunt double was there to catch him, but Kirk drove into him with such force that they both toppled over the side and fell on to the rocks below. Kirk smashed his head on a rock, which fortunately was relatively blunt. It opened a terrific gash in his head. 'How I didn't kill myself, I'll never know. I was lucky,' he says.

Kirk stayed on in Europe for his next production, *Catch Me A Spy*, although back in the States Bryna did produce *Summertree* for his son Michael to star in. *Catch Me A Spy* had Bryna co-producing with Ludgate Films of London and Capitole Films of Paris, and was shot in France and Scotland. The film, an off-beat spy story totally unlike any of the James Bond look-alikes, had the benefit of a fine screenplay written by one of Britain's best teams, Dick Clement and Ian La Frenais. Clement himself directed.

The film, completed in 1971, never received a major release in America. But Kirk needn't have worried. Europe as a whole was, and still is, just as important a film market as the United States. People can be superstars there without ever being seen in America. Charles Bronson had become the world's number one star simply by appearing in European pictures that were hardly seen in America or Britain.

So Kirk stayed on in Europe and went to Italy to set up another of his productions, this one called *A Man To Respect* (*Um Uomo Da Rispettare*). The film was a big success in Italy, with Kirk securing box office appeal by having as his co-stars top Italian stars Florinda Bolkan and Giuliano Gemma who was a sort of Italian Clint Eastwood. He then went to Yugoslavia and carried out the threat he'd been ominously making virtually since he started in movies. He was going to direct. 'I've always been accused of directing my films,' he joked. 'Now I can really be blamed.'

The picture he directed was *Scalawag*, another pirate adventure, but this time one he intended to be more in keeping with the pirates of traditional children's stories. He even wore a peg leg, since he was playing the title role himself. After all, he reasoned, how many actors could he get to be directed by him on his first attempt?

He gathered about him a cast of virtual children, most notably Lesley-Anne Down, then still almost unknown. He injected into the story the adventurous elements that had always thrilled him as a child. But the film was not a success. When I asked Kirk why he directed *Scalawag*, he told me, 'I'd thought about directing for a long time, but I kept hesitating, being afraid of it or whatever the reason was. So the first picture I tried to direct was *Scalawag* which I tried to make a very simple picture for children. I certainly learned a lot from it and had a lot of problems.

'But it was my first effort.'

It wouldn't be the last.

After *Scalawag*, Kirk went to England to attempt another new direction in his career. He was about to subtly send up his own image in *Cat And Mouse*. It was a picture he enjoyed making because it gave him the opportunity to show everybody that he really didn't take himself as seriously as everybody had always imagined he did. He said during its making in 1973:

> I'd call this a fun picture. I know the guy I play bumps off a couple of people. But he's so *interesting*. He's weak, and weakness is more interesting than strength. All the time I was playing tough guys strutting around owning the joint, I'd try and find something weak about them. If they didn't have a weak spot, I'd get bored with them.
>
> In the first films I made I played weak, drab men. And I sort of over-reacted against it. I was dying for a change of pace. So against everyone's advice I decided to play the tough hero in *Champion*. I succeeded too well. I became known as the toughest guy in Hollywood. What every actor wants to do is to work against the star system, and refuse to stay pigeon holed. With *Cat And Mouse* I've done that.

He at last returned to Hollywood and in 1974 he starred in *Once Is Not Enough*, based on Jaqueline Susann's sizzling sex novel, co-starring his son's live-in lover Brenda Vaccaro.

FOURTEEN/ One Last Western?

After *Once Is Not Enough*, in 1975 Kirk set about making what was for him his most important project since *Spartacus*. It was *Posse*, another western, but one in which he would reverse all the traditions of the classical western and introduce elements of contemporary history.

The reason for this film being made at this time is not far to seek.

The year 1975 was the time of great disillusionment in America. It was the era of the Watergate scandal. It was the time of political corruption made public. President Nixon was the hero who turned sour and earned the enmity of his people. Kirk, who was always loyal to the American flag, was just as disillusioned as the rest of the nation, but in his shock and outrage at what happened, he envisaged a film that would reflect today's news but in a period setting.

Based in the America of 1892, *Posse* features Douglas once again as a Marshal. And because it is Kirk Douglas, the audience quickly assumes that here is another heroic characterization standing for law and order. Marshal Douglas even intends running for State Senator, and as part of his election campaign he promises to bring to justice the notorious outlaw, personified by Bruce Dern.

During the late Sixties and throughout much of the Seventies, Bruce Dern had specialized in playing psychopaths and freaks. He had been thoroughly unlikeable in *Hang 'Em High*, in which he persuaded two boys to rustle cattle and got them hanged for it. In *Will Penny* he had helped to beat Charlton Heston almost to death. And, worst of all, in *The Cowboys* he killed John Wayne by shooting him in the back.

Now here he was being pursued by Kirk Douglas, whose posse has succeeded in massacring Dern's outlaw gang. So we know that Dern must be as dastardly and as evil as had previously been portrayed. But there is a switch. Douglas is so totally bent on winning his election that he uses the hunt for Dern as a political spotlight, and in the process displays his ambition and corruption. Dern, on the other hand, proves that there is honour even among thieves when he displays a more honest image than the Marshal's. He ends up capturing Douglas and holding him hostage, forcing the posse to restore the 40,000 dollars stolen money which they had taken from him. The posse now becomes like Sam Peckinpah's *Wild Bunch* when it loots a nearby town to get the money. The final irony comes when Dern allows the posse to share the money between them, so they in turn become outlaws leaving their corrupt and helpless Marshal to his own fate.

Not only did Kirk produce *Posse* through Bryna but he directed it also. It was a highly personal production for him in which he allowed himself to play the bad guy for once. It was also a production in which he redeemed himself of all previous displays of troublesome behaviour. On the set and throughout the pre-production stages, he was a total inspiration and the most malleable of film makers, though he never lacked the discipline to turn out a remarkable and thoroughly entertaining film.

Bruce Dern was full of praise for Kirk when I had the opportunity to talk with him:

> He was just unique. He made that film a lot of fun for us all to do. He really helped me in that movie. He just let me have a field day and gave me all kinds of interesting things to do.
>
> And he is a good director. *Posse* is a well directed picture. But it played only one week in America as the second half of a double bill. Can you believe that? It was a real good western, with a great twist at the end.

Kirk was equally full of praise for Dern:

> If I didn't have Bruce Dern playing that part, which he was perfect for, I would have had a lot of problems.
>
> I first saw him when we made *The War Wagon*. Bruce had a bit part then, but I watched him and was intrigued by him. I thought he had great humour as well as this tremendous menace which is what I wanted to use in *Posse*. I wanted to use that humour and that menace.
>
> I guess when we made *War Wagon* he thought I was kidding when I said, 'Someday I'm gonna get a good part for you.'

Posse was only Kirk's second attempt at directing. I asked him at the time of the film's release if he had been influenced by any particular director.

> I've been fortunate in that I've worked with a lot of good directors. But I'll probably never get to be as good as them.
>
> I've had directors like Mankiewicz, Kubrick, Wilder, Wyler, Hawks and Kazan. You certainly absorb, perhaps subconsciously, the things that you want to absorb and reject those you don't want.
>
> But as a director—or trying to be a director—my main thrust and concern was the actors. I think very often there's a tendency to say that a film is *the director's*, and that *he's* the genius. Well, how can anybody say it's *anybody's* film, when so many elements go into making pictures? It's a collaborative art. Certainly, the director probably has the dominant role. He's like a conductor conducting a symphony. If you've got a couple of bad violinists, I don't care how good a conductor you are, you've got a lot of problems. That's why I say I would've had a lot of problems if I hadn't had Bruce Dern.

So involved and concerned was Kirk in casting the right actors for the film that he even had the part of the town's newspaper editor especially written for the handicapped actor James Stacy. Stacy, who had recently lost an arm and a leg in

136

an accident, was virtually unemployable. But Kirk believed he had the right qualities for the role of the editor, and he had his screenplaywrights, William Roberts and Christopher Knopf, adapt the role for Stacy who could only get around on one crutch. This not only displayed Kirk's attentive method in casting but also his charitable attitude, because he hated to see Stacy out of work just because of his handicap.

Kirk's diligence as a movie producer is also amply exhibited in this picture. Very important to the story is the railroad and a train especially provided for the Marshal's dubious election methods. It becomes a means by which to hunt the outlaw as well as to proclaim his political intentions from. Kirk wasn't satisfied to use the typical western-style railroads usually available for film making purposes. He wanted something more than a train with a bit of track.

'Finding and using a suitable railway was a long, arduous process because the train plays a very important part in *Posse*,' he said. 'It had to be of course a train of the period, but I didn't want just a dull stretch of straight track. I looked around a long time before I found this piece of Southern Pacific Railroad track which had twists and turns and went around water and through a tunnel. But the Southern Pacific Railroad was very reluctant to let me use it for a movie. They didn't know what kind of condition they'd get it back in. So I had to do a lot of cajoling and pleading to get permission because I felt it was such a vital aspect of the picture.'

For Kirk the most important aspect of the picture was its statement on what basically was the Watergate affair. He told me proudly:

I wanted *Posse* to be an unusual western. Once we were inundated with westerns, especially on TV. Suddenly there were very few westerns being made, and I thought, 'You know, I'd like to make another western if I can find anything unusual.' And I certainly think *Posse* fits the bill. It shows a whole different character development, and yet it's filled with the classical elements of adventure that I think every western should have.

There was a wonderful time years ago—or as they say 'in the good old days'—when the good guys wore white

137

hats and the bad guys wore black hats. But today movies reflect the days we live in.

With Watergate and other things, suddenly the good guys are not very good, and the bad guys are not quite so bad. *Posse* reflects that. It's not a question of the bad guys trying to get the cattle or whatever. It's a very different character struggle between the Marshal and the outlaw.

I feel the worst kind of corruption is someone who supposedly defends the law, but is really a crook. I don't think a member of the Mafia is as guilty as a chief of police who turns out to be a crook, because the people have voted for the policeman assuming he's honest. The character I play in *Posse* has a nice image with the public and does a good job as a Marshal. But underneath his reason for wanting to become a Senator is sheer ambition. Yet I tried not to make him completely despicable. And then there's the outlaw played by Bruce Dern who has a peculiar set of ethics. He only robs trains! He's the lesser of the two evils.

Reminded of his first foray into directing, Kirk said, '*Scalawag* was my first effort. It was a cheap picture made in Europe. It hardly got seen anywhere. It wasn't very successful. I'd like to think that with *Posse* I've improved a great deal.'

He certainly had improved. *Posse* remains one of the best of the relatively few westerns made between the middle and late Seventies. In the UK the picture picked up some excellent reviews and did well at the box office. But in America the critics were harder to please, and as Bruce Dern said, it played only one week as a supporting feature, so insecure of it was Paramount who distributed it. But the problem wasn't with the film, but simply with the fact that suddenly westerns were not popular any more. Even John Wayne had given up riding the saddle to play a modern cop in films like *McQ* and *Brannigan*.

Probably for this reason among many others, Kirk Douglas announced that *Posse* would be his last western.

When I took this up with him, he said, 'Well I think of *Posse* as my last western, because I seem to have completed all the western periods, including a modern setting in *Lonely Are The Brave*, which is one of my favourite pictures. But in *Posse*, which is set in 1892, you're almost looking into the twentieth century, so I think of it as my last western.

'But then again, who knows? Maybe in a couple of years a western could come up that would excite me enough, but right now I can't think of doing another western after *Posse*.'

In leaving the wild West, for a period of a few years at least, Kirk would hit upon a genre of films that would provide him with his most successful period since the early days of Bryna. Fantasy and horror films were just around the corner.

FIFTEEN / The Rough and Broken Ground

Michael Douglas suffered one tremendous handicap: he could not escape the constant, virtually habitual press tag, 'Kirk Douglas's son'. Had he not been in the limelight, it wouldn't have mattered much since he would have been relatively unnoticed in the world. But he had chosen to become an actor, like dad, and comparisons were unavoidable. The mere fact that Michael was acting meant that he was constantly in the news, either in the daily press or fan magazines. And that meant that the readers were being updated on the 'son of Kirk Douglas'.

When Michael landed the secondary but plum role of Karl Malden's sidekick in the police series *The Streets Of San Francisco*, it was a big break for the son of Kirk. His films had not been particularly successful and if it hadn't been for the interest in his lineage, he would have provided little mileage for the publicity people or to the press. Naturally when he began making *The Streets Of San Francisco* he was still thought of as the offspring of his famous father, and it became a situation that seemed inescapable.

Michael concluded that if he was ever to make it on his own account, he needed to do something unique. Something that would actually overshadow anything his father had ever done. Certainly *The Streets Of San Francisco* went a long way to accomplishing that, since not even Kirk had ever had a TV series of his own.

'My father was impressed when I was doing the series because it was seen by twenty-two million people a week, every single week, in America alone,' recalls Michael.

Suddenly Michael was one of television's top stars. His popularity easily rivalled that of his father's even at Kirk's peak. It was something for Kirk's other sons to sit up and take notice of, much to Kirk's consternation.

'At least I never had to look at my father and think how am I going to make out as well as he does,' said Kirk. 'They all have the disadvantages of being Kirk Douglas's sons.'

Even with the success of *The Streets Of San Francisco*, though, Michael was still unable to shake off the 'son of' label. He was also informed by all the so-called experts that having become a television star, he would never make it big in movies.

It was true what Kirk had said. Michael did have the disadvantage of being Kirk Douglas's son. He had a lot to live up to because not only was his dad a famous actor, but he was also a successful producer. Michael was—had to be—in search of that elusive vehicle that would finally bring an end to his years of bondage by the press. He had to become Michael Douglas, the individual, and not the son of Kirk.

He succeeded in 1975.

As Kirk explains it, 'For fifteen years I tried to put on the movie of *One Flew Over The Cuckoo's Nest*. I had played it on Broadway for five months or so and felt it would make a great movie. I took it to every studio head in town. Everybody said that it wouldn't work. I owned the film rights, and Michael said, "Let me have it."

'Well, he succeeded in getting it made because the time was right. Sometimes your instinct is right, but the time is wrong. But he made the project the great classic that it is today.'

Many years later Kirk made a film based on an Australian poem, *The Man From Snowy River*, which told how a boy became a man by outriding the experienced horseman 'through stringy-barks and saplings on the rough and broken ground'.

At that later time, looking back at his son's success, Kirk said, 'The Man From Snowy River in my family is my son Michael. He wanted to take the play of *Cuckoo's Nest* and ride with it "on the rough and broken ground". And he did. He out-rode me. He became a man.'

Michael never even appeared in the film of *One Flew Over The Cuckoo's Nest*. The part Kirk had played on the stage went to Jack Nicholson who won an Oscar for his performance. Michael was purely an off-screen performer, functioning for the first time in his life as a film producer. He had, of course, had much behind-the-scenes experience, having worked in various capacities on some of his father's films. He didn't even direct *Cuckoo's Nest*; and one almost forgets that it was Milos Foreman who had that particular task. Today one tends immediately to think of the name Michael Douglas in connection with that film.

The ironic thing was that Michael's success as an actor in *The Streets Of San Francisco* made him one of the best-known producers around at the time of *Cuckoo's Nest*'s release.

Michael recalls, 'When we got off the plane in Japan to promote *Cuckoo's Nest*, Jack Nicholson was shocked that all the reporters swarmed around *me*. After all, he was the star and I was the producer, but *The Streets Of San Francisco* had been running there for a couple of years!'

One Flew Over The Cuckoo's Nest was an unqualified success, raking in millions at the box office, and confirmed Michael's status as a major Hollywood film producer. Of course, his father had been a successful producer for many years, but Michael had actually succeeded where Kirk had failed. He had managed to not only produce a film version of *Cuckoo's Nest*, but he had turned it into a money-spinner and a classic. And it won the Best Picture Oscar which went to Michael.

Suddenly Michael Douglas was no longer being called the son of Kirk in every news item that appeared about him. Kirk recalls with good humour an incident that once occurred to him. 'A pretty girl ran up to me on a plane with a lovely look in her eye. I started to congratulate myself. Then she asked me, "Hey, are you really Michael Douglas's father?"'

'I'm delighted at Michael's success. I want all my sons to surpass me, because that's a form of immortality.'

There is no doubt that Michael's achievement as a producer of films, and the progressive stability in his private life, have contributed immensely to the closeness Kirk now enjoys with him. It has always been important to Kirk to have his family united. 'We're not together as often as we like,' says Kirk, 'because we're all usually travelling some place. But family reunions are great.'

One of the family's favourite sports is tennis. At Kirk's second home in Palm Springs, he has a tennis court where the family occasionally congregates. There the boys all take turns in challenging dad. 'They really like trying to beat the stuffing out of their old man,' says Kirk. Tennis has long been one of Kirk's favourite pastimes. He particularly enjoys the occasions when professional players drop by for a game. Kirk recalls one particular time when Nastase came round, having just been disqualified. He spent all afternoon teaching Anne how to improve her backhand. 'Just having him round was a thrill for me,' says Kirk. 'I'm still turned on by real class. If you've got class, you're the richest guy in the world.'

And Kirk is certainly that, in all ways. He is a millionaire movie star, but he never spends a lot of money on material things. As he says, 'I've tried not to let the trappings of fame rule my life.' Even the house he has in Beverly Hills is modest in comparison to other Hollywood stars' homes. He has, however, used his wealth to decorate his home with art. He is a keen collector, and owns original paintings by Rouault, Picasso, Chagall and Vlaminck. The family pulls his leg because he owns no Van Gogh paintings. 'I can't afford one,' he says, adding, 'besides, I'd have the feeling I'd painted it myself.'

Few pictures of movie stars hang in his home. Instead there is an abundance of photographs featuring royalty and important politicians, many of them autographed. He treasures a number of photographs of Presidents John F. Kennedy and Lyndon B. Johnson. It is, as would be expected, a comfortable home, but Kirk refuses to fill his wardrobe to overflowing or buy countless cars. Peter often tells him he ought to splurge just for the hell of it. At such times Kirk is apt to remind his sons about his childhood and how he and his six sisters had virtually nothing. He once recounted for them the time he had found a potato and had cooked it over a fire and shared it with a friend. One of his sons responded with, 'You're absolutely right, dad. It's time I suffered a little. Tell you what. I'll go and steal a potato, light a fire on a sidewalk in Beverly Hills and see how long it takes before I'm arrested.'

Kirk concedes that in fact his sons have it tougher in many ways than he ever did. 'They suffer in other ways,' he says. 'For a start, it can't be easy for any of them having a famous father who's in the same line of business they all want to be in.' Kirk would never give up, though, telling them that he had it toughest overall.

In time all his sons would begin carving out successful careers for themselves in the movie business, much to Kirk's alarm since he always warned them against going into the picture business. He had seen how hard Michael had had it. But as the years rolled by, Kirk watched with glowing pride as his oldest boy went from strength to strength, both professionally and personally. Michael wanted to involve himself more in movies and so he made the decision to quit *The Streets Of San Francisco*. He was becoming, like his father, a gambler.

'All my life I've been brought up with the myth that if you were on a television series you had to wait a long time for a film career,' says Michael. 'I kept hearing, "If audiences can see you on television, why would they pay to see you in a movie?"

'Well, it is just a myth and recently it's been getting the stuffing kicked out of it. Going back some, a lot of film stars like Steve McQueen, Clint Eastwood, George C. Scott, James Coburn and Burt Reynolds all got started on television. And recently John Travolta, Henry Winkler and Chevy Chase too.'

Michael was still keen to act but he also wanted to produce. He was keen to set up a picture in which he could star and involve himself in the production, and he knew it would have to be something extraordinary so that he really could blow his TV image for good. He came up with *The China Syndrome* in 1979, and in making it, he went into partnership with Jane Fonda, who was also into producing her own pictures by this time and being a success at it too. The film told the controversial story of a leak at a nuclear power station which threatened to result in a horrifying holocaust. The film, which also co-starred Jack Lemmon alongside of Fonda and Douglas, was a sensational hit, made all the more outstanding when the film's release coincided with a real-life nuclear crisis on Three Mile Island in America.

Some movie observers claimed the film was making the statement that nuclear power should be banned. Kirk was put on the spot as an unwilling spokesman and he gave his own point of view on the subject. 'I vote for nuclear power,' he announced. 'It's already here. It's here to stay. The film Jane and Michael have made says that it's got to be watched over more carefully. I don't disagree. But I think we're more likely to have a nuclear war over an oil shortage.'

Kirk did his best to stay out of the limelight during the film's release. After all, he had nothing to do with it and besides which, he said, 'I'm not one of those Hollywood stars who uses celebrity to make political statements.'

The truth was he wasn't in total harmony with Jane Fonda and her radical views and behaviour. During the Vietnam War she had tried to gather together a contingent of Hollywood actors to go to Hanoi and sign their own separate peace treaty with the Communists. When she approached Kirk about this, he told her, 'Isn't that something we'd better leave to our senators?' He never heard from her again.

Now that his film career was really taking off, Michael was eager to put his private life into some semblance of normality. He had broken up with Brenda Vaccaro before making *The China Syndrome*. While the film was still in its development, Michael had attended a pre-Inaugural party in honour of President Carter. There were hundreds of other figures from the world of entertainment at the event in Washington, DC. There was also an abundance of diplomats representing countries from all around the world, and with them were members of their families.

Among these was twenty-year-old Diandra Luker, a beauty from Majorca and daughter of a Spanish diplomat. She was in the process of completing her last year at Georgetown University in the foreign service programme. All she knew about was the political and international social world. She knew nothing about Michael Douglas, who introduced himself to her. He had then a beard which he wore for the film, and she thought him very handsome. She thought he was perhaps an artist, but when he explained that he was an actor, she was quite disappointed. She'd hardly seen any films and had certainly never seen *The Streets Of San Francisco*. She had been educated at Swiss boarding schools where all the students were limited to just one hour of French television a week. She hadn't even seen a movie until she was in her teens.

The day after their meeting, Michael asked Diandra to lunch, and over the coming weeks Michael flew back and forth from New York to Washington, concentrating on his work in the East but also on courting Diandra in the West.

When his work in New York was complete, he returned to California. To Diandra's complete surprise, he asked her to marry him and live in California. She accepted.

They were married in 1977 while Michael was immersed in production on *The China Syndrome*. He even managed to find her a small part in the film, playing a production assistant at the television station where Jane Fonda's character works as a reporter. In 1979 Diandra gave birth to baby Cameron, turning a delighted Kirk Douglas into a grandfather at the age of sixty-three. Michael's marriage and the start of a family brought about a great change in Michael. 'After two years of marriage,' he says, 'including becoming a father, I know that my marriage is of utmost importance to me. Unexpectedly, marriage has helped me clarify my goals, assess my priorities, and work with more energy and effectiveness than ever before.'

It was a change of heart which Kirk had always been hoping and praying for. He had seen his son struggling for an identity which had sent him fleeing to a hippy commune to live in the kind of squalor which Kirk had always fought hard to escape from. Over the years Kirk had stood on the sidelines and watched his son grow in wisdom and stature, and now at last he had seen his son not so much conform to what Kirk considered to be normal but find a reason for being that way.

'Being a parent has given me a whole sense of continuity through the family structure,' said Michael. 'It has made me realize that the only threads we have left in society is the family structure. Hopefully, people are getting back into being parents and enjoying it. Besides providing a strong base of love and security for my child, I would like specifically to encourage the development of willpower, stamina and discpline. Like physical exercise, those skills must be attained little by little over the years.'

Although there was great fulfillment and satisfaction in the lives of Michael and Diandra, there was unhappiness too. Most of Michael's friends refused to accept Diandra after he and Brenda split up. It was a situation which drove him ever closer to his father who himself had always suffered from lack of friends. 'I've been told that I'm bad news as a friend,' says Kirk. 'They've said I was like a steamship ploughing through, and if people hung on, they hung on and hoped they didn't get thrown off. I think it's caused me a lot of loneliness. What people do not realize, probably because of my image and appearance, is that often I'm really very shy and insecure. That's why my wife is so important to me. I make her my friend and someone to talk to, because I don't have many friends. A lot of the loneliness stems from not knowing whom to trust. I think of someone like John Travolta. You can have one big picture, two bad pictures, and they kick you straight up the backside. I know.'

It was his knowledge of just how hard the movie business could be on any individual that always prompted Kirk to try and dissuade his sons from wanting to be in movies. But even young Eric was by about this time taking up much of his time at college with acting and directing plays. Kirk did his best to push him in other areas. 'Are you taking courses in economics?' he'd ask Eric. 'How about a business degree?'

Kirk would have a fight on his hands with all his sons. But then Kirk had always been a fighter. He can battle with wits and with words. Physically, he avoids any confrontation.

Somewhat to his consternation—or perhaps just good humour—he found during his travels to London during the Seventies that the press were beginning to write articles about him that were in complete contrast to his tough guy image. When one woman reporter wrote that Kirk Douglas turned out to be a nice, bright, intelligent guy and not at all what she had expected, Kirk wrote to her the following day and, para- phrased, he said, 'How dare you deliberately set out to ruin a reputation built on years of rumour and hearsay? If you ever say another nice thing about me again, I'll sue you!' Kirk insisted that his career 'couldn't take the terrible knocks my belligerent tough guy image had been taking recently'. He is at least honest about it all.

'Actually, I have been pretty aggressive in my time,' he says. 'I was born aggressive, and I guess I'll die aggressive. It's the only way to survive in show business. But what I do have is compassion. Nobody ever writes about the new talent I try to encourage. If I have any vice at all, it's a king-sized ego.'

SIXTEEN/ New Trends, New Successes

On 27 June 1976, the world was shaken when an Air Force jumbo jet was hijacked by four terrorists on its flight over Greece and forced to land at Entebbe Airport in Uganda. Among the passengers were 103 Jews, all of whom became the 'guests' of President Amin and the hostages of Arab terrorists. Then, on 4 July, the world was elated by the almost unbelievable news that an Israeli commando unit had made a surprise raid on Entebbe Airport and overcome the Ugandan guards and the terrorists, rescuing the Jews who were undoubtedly otherwise on a course for extermination. It was one of the most daring and courageous rescue operations in history. Planned down to the most minute details and executed with ice-cool courage and efficiency, it was an impossible mission which proved triumphant.

Within just a few days of the raid taking place, television producer Robert Grunette and writer Ernest Kinoy were in Israel, researching the amazing story which was about to inspire no fewer than three film versions. But the first off the ground was Grunette's production, which actually wasn't a film but a taped production. With the backing of Warner Bros, he was able to assemble an impressive cast of American and British stars. Among these were Anthony Hopkins as the Israeli Prime Minister, Richard Dreyfuss as the commander of the operation, Burt Lancaster as the Minister of Defence,

Linda Blair as an Israeli hostage, Elizabeth Taylor as an anxious mother, and as her equally worried husband there was Kirk Douglas.

Douglas had always maintained that he wasn't interested in playing cameo parts. But something from his Jewish ancestry stirred when he read Ernest Kinoy's marvellous teleplay. The raid—codenamed Operation Thunderbolt—was enough to restore all the pride and zeal of the Children of Israel, and Kirk wanted to do his part in honouring the Israeli commandos and the government for their achievement. But he didn't choose to play a role in which he would be featured as one of the great heroes of the raid or one of the backroom military brains as did Burt Lancaster.

Kirk chose to portray a man who represented the Israeli people, who at the time were concerned for the welfare of their families and friends held hostage in Uganda. He confronts Anthony Hopkins as the Prime Minister, demanding to know what the authorities are doing to rescue his young daughter. The casting of Elizabeth Taylor as his wife was also something of a coup, but she like Kirk was stirred and inspired by the story of Jewish courage. She had been converted herself to Judaism when she married the late Mike Todd.

It was Kirk's first television production and one in which he enjoyed the luxury of not having to fly out to some distant location since the whole programme was taped at Warner Bros' television studios. Then a peculiar thing happened. In a race to be the first to bring the story of Entebbe to the cinema screen, Warner Bros took their superb television production, which was called appropriately *Victory At Entebbe*, abridged it and transferred the tape to film and released it as a movie. The results were disastrous. Video tape does not transfer successfully to film, and much of the dramatic sweep of the original was lost. It was quickly overshadowed by the second version of the operation, Columbia's *Raid On Entebbe*, which was initially made for television also,—Columbia, though, had the foresight to film it as opposed to taping it.

(For the record, the third version, an Israeli production proudly called *Entebbe—Operation Thunderbolt*, was released too long after the event and the release of the previous two pictures, and was all but ignored.)

Although *Victory At Entebbe* was not a box office hit, which initially it was never intended to be anyway, it was successful on television, and Kirk at last discovered what it felt like to know that 20 or 30 million viewers all over America were watching you at one time. It gave him a thrill, and he determined to do more television if he could just find the right material.

Meanwhile, a whole new trend had been taking place in the cinema. It all began with Linda Blair who had portrayed Kirk's daughter in the *Entebbe* teleplay. Linda Blair had shot to international stardom just a few years previously in the grotesque and grossly evil film, *The Exorcist*. It was a sensational hit, featuring scenes of vomiting, masturbation using a crucifix, blood, gore—the lot. Technically brilliant and for a while the most successful film of all time, it spawned a whole spate of devil movies and films about the supernatural that could now feature the kind of gratuitous scenes which today make those old Hammer horror classics look positively tame.

Kirk astutely recognized the commercial value of such films and knew that if he wanted another movie hit, the best bet was to flow with the tide. He chose to make a devil movie. It was *Holocaust 2000*, an Italian production directed by Alberto DeMartino though filmed in part in England. This was a whole new departure for Kirk who enjoyed the experience of filming in Wykehurst Park, a huge spooky mansion in Sussex, where *The Legend Of Hell House*, another successful horror movie, had been shot. Kirk played an industrial magnate who decides to build a thermo-nuclear plant in a Third World country. But when his plans spark a series of seemingly demonic events, he is pushed to the borders of insanity while the world edges closer to destruction. It was above all a devil picture, with Simon Ward portraying Satan in the guise of Kirk's son.

Typically, Kirk also found a more contemporary and realistic reason for making *Holocaust 2000*: 'This film is based on a very serious problem,' he said during the film's production which, incidentally, came before his son Michael's production of *The China Syndrome*:

It's the construction of thermo-nuclear plants. I don't think there's a day goes by in which you don't pick up a newspaper and read the pros and cons about thermo-nuclear plants, about the dangers involved, how safe they can be made, what happens if small countries have the means of making atomic weapons, and so on.

The film combines this very serious contemporary problem with biblical predictions of the Apocalypse and that a seven-headed monster from the Anti-Christ would come out of the sea and destroy humanity.

It's a very provocative movie and has tremendous suspense and mystery. Anyone opposing the construction of these thermo-nuclear plants always meets with a violent accident. I'm enjoying it all immensely.

Kirk has always maintained that he likes to make pictures which have a message, but that it is pointless if it isn't done in an entertaining way. 'There is no point in making a movie,' he says, 'if you don't aim to make it commercial.' *Holocaust 2000* had a message about thermo-nuclear plants, but Kirk also knew that the Satanic elements would bring in the audiences.

By now Kirk was sixty-one though still extremely vital and active. But he was finding the chore of producing, and especially directing, growing heavy. He had made a conscious decision only to act in future. 'I prefer to work now as an actor,' he said. 'I used to produce and act all the time. I like working on the script, getting ideas. But I no longer want the responsibility of being a producer.'

Before leaving Hollywood to make *Holocaust 2000* Kirk had told Peter, 'It's wonderful. I'm going on this picture and I'm just going to be an actor.'

'Dad,' said Peter, 'you could never be *just* an actor.'

'I must be involved,' says Kirk. 'In everything. I love the business too much. And an actor is always looking for *that* part, no matter how many roles he's played.

'I feel lucky, more and more each year. I'm very fortunate. For thirty years to be doing what I wanted to do is pretty good going. It's like having a party and never completely growing up.

'To be an actor you have to retain a certain childishness. If you become so sophisticated you'd say to yourself, "How could I pretend to be a cowboy shooting it out with Burt Lancaster?

Grown men playing at cowboys! What a crazy way to make a living." If I thought like that I'd be finished.'

Devil movies are notorious for so-called jinx experiences. Kirk isn't himself a superstitious man, but there was one incident when making *Holocaust 2000* which unnerved him and shook him up. He was involved in a scene in which he had to do nothing more complicated than drive a Rolls Royce car through the gates of Wykehurst Park. Now here was the man who had ridden his horse into the midst of a cohort of Roman legionnaires; who had stormed a castle Viking style; who'd manoeuvred difficult wagons across the Oregon Trail. And all he had to do was drive a car.

Somehow he managed to take a right turn too sharply, and he smashed the Rolls into a camera team. The Rolls and the camera sustained 100,000 dollars worth of damage. Kirk emerged from the car shaken and concerned for the camera team. He went straight to the men behind the camera and found to his relief none of them was hurt. He tried his best to show concern, but nobody else seemed a bit bothered. They all ended up laughing about it.

'It was beautiful creaming that Rolls and the camera,' said Kirk. 'I mean, it doesn't happen every day, does it?'

Although he recognized the trend in these horror pictures in time to cash in on them, he still valued some of his more traditional territories. Despite what he had said, in 1977 he was planning to make yet another western, called *Draw*, and hoped to make it with his pal Burt Lancaster. He also had aspirations of appearing on the London stage, again with Lancaster. Both dreams would be realized in the future, though not quite in full.

While he was waiting to fulfil these ambitions, Kirk was allowing himself to be seduced by television. Just a couple of years previously, *Rich Man, Poor Man* had hit the TV screens as four hour-and-a-half episodes. It was the first of the 'miniseries' which usually ran under the heading *Best Sellers*—the American studios found gold in transcribing best-selling novels into these slick, glossy mini-series.

Such mini-series succeeded in casting big-name movie stars who generally wouldn't have touched television. The usual run-of-the-mill American TV shows tied actors up day in, day out for months at a time, and often had them bogged down in the same TV series for years. So most movie stars avoided them like the plague. But these mini-series were something else. They were made faster than motion pictures, but not as fast as the orthodox TV series, and they didn't tie any actor down for the rest of his working life.

Kirk Douglas had been on the lookout for a suitable television project following *Victory At Entebbe*, and found it in *The Moneychangers*, a first-class mini-series. It was a glimpse behind the scenes of banking and the world of high finance, coupled with the soap-opera lives of bankers and business men and women. 'Everybody watched it,' he was able to later say with much glee. 'And they were all talking about it. I guess the fascination was money. We're all interested in that. We're always in and out of banks, but we never really know what goes on behind the banks' closed doors.

'It was quite an experience working in television. I was staggered at the pace. This old man's used to taking things steady on film sets. But I enjoyed it.'

He also continued to enjoy acting as the State Department's official goodwill ambassador, and during 1977 he travelled to England, Italy and Israel. It was in the land of his ancient forefathers that he came to comprehend the power of a TV series like *The Moneychangers*. He was virtually unable to step outside of his hotel without being mobbed by fans. Not even in the United States or Great Britain was he actually mobbed anymore, but in Israel he was something of a hero, no doubt due to his Jewish blood and his portrayal of great Israeli heroes such as Mickey Marcus in *Cast A Giant Shadow* and the Israeli man-next-door in *Victory At Entebbe*. It was while he was in Israel that *The Moneychangers* was being aired there. It was then he discovered that he could walk the streets at night almost unnoticed, because just about the whole population was indoors watching *The Moneychangers*.

Kirk stayed with the commercial market for his next picture, *The Fury*, a psychic thriller directed by Brian de Palma who established for himself a reputation as the Hitchcock of the Seventies with a number of thrillers and terror pictures like *Phantom Of The Paradise*, *Obsession* and most notably *Carrie*. The last-named picture was a terrifying classic about psychic phenomena and hysteria: *The Fury* was to be very much in the same vein.

Co-starring with Kirk in this tale of psychic twins was the young, lovely and unknown Amy Irving, who later came to fame in the blockbusting television mini-series, *The Far Pavilions*. A dedicated serious young actress, she studied acting for four years in London because she felt that she would learn far more about the craft there than anywhere in America. When she began working on *The Fury* she was immediately ill at ease with Kirk. He was telling her how to play her part, which she resented on impulse. She was usually confident about her own abilities and ideas. She now suddenly found herself working alongside an old pro who not only gave her advice which she felt she didn't need, but whose very stature and aggressive attitude was enough to make her feel three feet small.

In an interview at the time of the release of *The Fury*, Amy Irving told me:

> I was intimidated by him at first. He came in and he had all his own ideas, and to him I was just this new person. I am outspoken but I felt it wasn't all right to speak my mind with him. So I held back for a while, but Brian de Palma always encouraged me to come out with it because he wants to hear if I have something to say. Kirk would try teaching me. He said, 'Don't spend half an hour working yourself up into an hysterical state before you do a scene. Take three minutes or you're going to kill yourself before this movie is over. You have a lot of high-energy scenes to do. You can do it in three minutes.'
>
> And I would think, 'Well, I've trained for four years, I know my own techniques.'
>
> But after a week of me running around and screaming and being in that constant state of fear and hysteria, I said to him, 'Kirk, you were right,' and I started doing just like he said.
>
> Kirk and I ended up being able to work very closely together. He has so much energy, but he's a pussy cat. The man never ceases to amaze me.

He certainly was something of an amazing man. Then sixty-two, he was incredibly fit and slim, a fact which many critics when reviewing *The Fury* didn't fail to notice.

'I bicycle five miles every day and keep myself pretty fit,'

Kirk was able to boast. 'But I'm beginning to be concerned. When *The Fury* was reviewed it read like a physical fitness report. *Kirk Douglas looking tremendously well — Kirk Douglas showing remarkable energy — Kirk Douglas incredibly vigorous*. If it goes on like this, soon they'll be saying, *Kirk Douglas, pulse rate so and so, blood count so and so!*'

Kirk could afford to laugh. *Holocaust 2000* and *The Fury* were proving to be his most successful pictures in years, and because he was big box office again, movie producers were queueing up at his front door with offers of major Hollywood films. Again Kirk decided to play safe following a trend. It was now the era of the science fiction epic. *Star Wars* had broken new boundaries in exploring a fantastic universe, and so began a cycle of space-age films that were generally more sophisticated than and technically superior to the majority of previous sci-fi efforts.

It was only natural that Kirk should want a sci-fi blockbuster, and so when veteran Hollywood producer Stanley Donen offered Kirk the lead in *Saturn 3*, he grabbed it hungrily. Again it brought Kirk back to England where the film was made under close wraps at Shepperton Studios. It had become usual when making these expensive futuristic adventures for the makers to try and outdo each other with the special effects and technical hardware they'd be using. The set of *Saturn 3* was like Fort Knox. No one got on it unless they were involved with the movie. There was something which Stanley Donen was keeping secret. One was the fact that after a disagreement of some kind with the film's director, Donen was now helming the shooting on the set without actually receiving credit for it. But the other great secret was in the shape of Hector, an amazing robot which walked, talked and did just about everything, including ripping off the head of co-star Harvey Keitel and placing it on his own mechanical body.

Kirk had the additional benefit of having *Charlie's Angel* Farrah Fawcett as his leading lady. She was then at her peak and a totally gorgeous creature in the rather seductive space-age underwear she wore in the film. Because no one was able to get a glimpse of Hector at work, everyone naturally focused their full attention on Kirk and Farrah, and in particular a nude love scene they share. There was also a sequence in which

Kirk fights completely naked with Harvey Keitel, displaying an almost full-frontal and a total bare rear view. There was no doubt, despite Kirk's obvious annoyance with the critics' obsession about his physical condition in *The Fury*, that he was now giving his trim figure a big screen exhibition which again had everyone marvelling at his physique considering he was now sixty-three.

'I try to stay in shape during the making of a film,' he said. 'I get the proper rest, eat the right things. There are no roles for fat leading men! There's nothing that I can't do now that I used to do when I was twenty—I just don't do it as often! It's mainly a question of common sense and willpower. I always stand when most people sit, run when most walk, and walk when most people ride.'

Kirk's co-star Farrah was certainly feeling the pressure of stardom, something which Kirk had long learned to cope with. The main difference between them was that Farrah was, coming from a plastic television series, something of a manufactured star, and she was desperate to try and prove that she was a real actress. Kirk recognized this and was very protective of her. He tried to help her in any way he could, knowing that she had far more at stake in this picture than he did.

'Farrah's very relaxed and easy to work with,' he said when making *Saturn 3*. 'We get on well together. She definitely has a great talent, though you have to push her sometimes. But there is much more depth to Farrah than anyone has given her credit for, or any opportunity to show.'

Kirk got a great kick out of playing a spaceman astronaut. It was something he had never had the opportunity, or desire, to do before. But now he said, 'I'm looking for new challenges in acting. Maybe it's senility setting in, being a child again, because acting is a childish profession.'

Saturn 3 was a long time in the making. Much of the time was spent getting the robot to perform correctly. This gave Kirk the opportunity to get away from the studios and talk about films. In fact, he enjoys discussing films with the English probably more than with any other people in the world. He told me:

> In England I am so amazed because I've never seen a country where people know so much about movies. I have

a secretary in London who's worked with me quite a bit, and she knows much more about my movies than I do. If somebody says to me, 'In what year did you do that movie?' and I say, 'I don't know,' she'd know immediately.

I find a lot of real movie buffs here. They've studied more than in America, maybe because we're so close to Hollywood.

SEVENTEEN/
Just For the Fun of It

Kirk always takes his work seriously; he has learned to take himself much less seriously.

Judging by the hard-nosed, temperamental, egotistical image which he has evolved, you'd think the last thing he'd be amused at is anyone taking the rise out of him. But in fact he loves it. He gets a big kick out of watching in particular impressionist Frank Gorshin who does the slickest, funniest, most accurate impersonation of Kirk Douglas. Gorshin's act usually has him doubling as both Douglas and Burt Lancaster. In fact, other than his portrayal of the Riddler in the *Batman* series, Gorshin's impressions of Douglas and Lancaster are what he is best known for.

Gorshin successfully captures the whole essence of Kirk Douglas, by exaggerating both his best and worst points. In this way, Kirk believes, Gorshin and other such mimics do him a service. Gorshin particularly highlights Kirk's intensity with jutting chin, lips drawn back at the corners and a voice that seems to wallow in anguish. Kirk says, 'My intensity is one of my strengths but it is also a weakness. I try to look at my work with a critical eye and I sometimes find an over-abundance of intensity.' It is by studying the way Gorshin mimics him that he learns—or tries—to subdue that intensity when it's not needed, or any other aspect of his performance.

But having accepted that mimics pick on his intensity so that

159

it is exaggerated to the point where it is hilarious, Kirk himself is apt to go around the house mimicking Gorshin mimicking him. He calls it 'coming on heavy as Kirk Douglas'.

His boys, however, are usually unimpressed.

'Gorshin does it better,' they tell him.

Deciding it was time that he in fact did it better, he played in the spoof western *Cactus Jack*. It was a film which succeeded brilliantly in its visual jokes, most of them being based on the Road Runner and Coyote cartoons, but failed in its dialogue. Nevertheless, it is an intriguing film to watch just to see how much Kirk is obviously enjoying himself at sending himself up.

He plays Cactus Jack, the lousiest villain in the West. He waits patiently upon a rock which overlooks the railway, waiting for the train to pass. When it does, he leaps off the rock like Butch Cassidy, only the slow-motion camera keeps him hanging in air too long, and the train whizzes by, leaving him to crash to the ground. Kirk said:

> It's a role I felt I had to do, just for the fun of it. Cactus Jack is one of those people who simply aren't cut out for their jobs. He's rotten enough to be a villain. And he certainly looks the part, dressed in black leather with a pencil-line moustache, astride a black horse. But the nastier he gets, the more things go wrong. It's not obvious casting. Y'see, the first temptation with a property like this is to cast a comedian. But if a well-known comic had played Cactus Jack Slade, you'd know up front that he was going to get into funny situations and how he would handle them. Kirk Douglas can spring a few surprises.
>
> This film is wild, insane, off-the-wall humour. Looking back over my career, I doubt that many producers or directors would have pictured me in the role. I'm not even sure that *I* would have thought of me. But Mort Engleberg the producer did, and so did my director Hal Needham, and I'm grateful because I've had so much fun.

Adding to the fun were Ann-Margret as Charming Jones and hulk-like Arnold Schwarzenegger playing Handsome Stranger some years before he became a star as *Conan the Barbarian*. The plot of *Cactus Jack* has Charming and Handsome carrying a strongbox of gold in their buckboard. It's Jack's job to get it from them. Just like the cartoon character Coyote, he tries swinging down at them from trees, rolling huge rock boulders down hills at them, even painting a false cave on the side of the mountain. But each time, Cactus Jack is the one flattened by the boulder or who goes running into the side of the mountain while Charming and Handsome have somehow managed to ride straight through the false cave.

These are jokes which work wonderfully and make the film so plain entertaining. It even has the classic cartoon joke where Cactus Jack pours glue over the railway track where the buckboard must pass: when it goes straight over without getting stuck, Cactus Jack steps his foot in it to test it. Naturally, *he* gets stuck, and finds himself in the way of the approaching train.

For the filming of this sequence, Kirk insisted on doing one risky shot himself in which he is stuck on the front of the locomotive as it speeds along.

'I've always resented actors who leave all the hard work to doubles,' he said. 'I got a big kick out of the scene where I had to be tied to the front of the speeding locomotive. Hal Needham couldn't have shot the scene the way he did if it hadn't been me up there.'

It was very much a stuntman's film, and Kirk did have to leave many of the more dangerous feats to the professional stunt men. But he was always able to get the go-ahead from Needham whenever he considered it safe enough for Kirk to do it himself. And Needham should know. 'Hal was my stunt double in *The War Wagon*, *The Way West* and *In Harm's Way*. Now he's my director and I've loved it,' said Kirk.

There was one moment when, during filming, Kirk did have to stop and think for a minute about some of the daring stunts he was performing:

I was climbing down a mountain and getting smashed around when somebody said, 'Why work so hard? You're a rich man.' It brought me up short. I said, 'Well, I enjoy it.' I couldn't think of any other answer. Work is tied up with being alive.

Movie making is a draining experience and without health you just can't function, not in art and not in life. I approach a new picture like an athlete approaches a sports event.

In making *Cactus Jack* Kirk broke his own rule about making no more westerns, although he was already planning to make *Draw* at some time, but he felt perfectly justified in making this comical western. 'It was about time I made fun of myself,' he said. 'After all, every impersonator in the business has been doing it for years.'

Away from the screen, Kirk was concentrating more on his private life. Now heading for his mid-sixties, he seemed satisfied to make fewer films than he had been used to. He had stopped producing and although there had been a time when he wanted to direct so desperately, he was satisfied just to be part of the creative process as an actor.

'Movie making is complicated,' he says, 'because a film is the result of a co-operative effort. Unlike a painter, a writer, a composer, you can't ever say, "This is *my* work," because you haven't done it all alone by yourself. Now I'm learning how to do *nothing*. I was never able to do nothing. What I mean is reading a book, relaxing by the pool, not getting involved in anything. It's a wonderful feeling that recharges the batteries.'

At an age when most people were already into planning for their retirement, Kirk shrugged off any notion of becoming an old age pensioner. 'Me retire?' he explodes. 'Never! I feel compelled to work. By doing *nothing*, I only mean *once in a while*. I must do a movie, be on stage, write a book, *anything*. It's part of me, part of breathing. It's my life.'

EIGHTEEN/
An Incurable
Disease

Michael Douglas took one long look at his dad who stood lean, strong and as fit as any man half his age. Then Michael considered his own plump shape. 'I'm only thirty-three and Kirk is making me look bad,' he said. He had never learned to take care of himself the way dad had. And now his appearance was beginning to show it. 'I was a bit of a toad in *The China Syndrome*, and grew the beard to hide my double chin,' said Michael. 'I was so debauched. I'd be into character acting if I didn't watch it.'

So he started to watch it. He found the motivation when he starred in a picture called *Running*, in which he played a marathon runner. Now he had to get into condition. He rose each day at 6.30 and went running up and down the Beverly Hills canyons, first for twenty minutes each day and later for up to ninety minutes a day. He gave up cigarettes, and he lost twelve pounds.

There had been a time when Michael had dropped right out of life because he felt he couldn't compete with his father. But now he wanted to compete. He knew he might never surpass his dad, but he just wanted to be in there and running. It was now also the same with Kirk's other sons. Peter and Joel were already into producing movies, and worst of all Eric was so determined to be an actor, he had managed to gain acceptance into RADA, much to Kirk's consternation.

He thought about Eric starting in dramatic school, and he thought, 'Oh Jeez, I just can't go through all that again.' He knew of the disappointments, of the parts that you felt you deserved but never got. 'Film making is the saddest profession in the world,' he would constantly remind his sons, 'because too many things go wrong, so many disappointments creep into your life. But you can't get out of it. It's like an incurable disease once you're in this business.'

He always discouraged his sons from coming into the business, but he also knew that his sons' careers stemmed directly from that sense of competition which had always been there between him and his boys. Every family has a sense of competition. He knew that. But he knew that it was more difficult in his business where everything is so much larger than life. Now the competition had spread, because his younger sons weren't just competing with him, they were competing with Michael too. Michael had escaped the tag 'son of Kirk' and now Peter, Joel and Eric didn't want to be known as 'brothers of Michael'.

Kirk now started to look upon Michael's experience as being much different to the experiences that Peter, Joel and Eric were going through. 'I'm proud of the way Michael's handled his success,' says Kirk, 'but I think it's because he has gone through a lot that he's able to handle it.' His other sons, he felt, were virtually starting at the top. Joel, for instance, had jumped in at the deep end and produced a picture called *King Cobra*. It was a small but nevertheless major film. But even more startling was Peter, who chose for his first picture a multi-million-dollar fantasy war epic, *The Final Countdown*.

It was the story of the nuclear aircraft carrier USS *Nimitz*, which finds itself back in the days of the Second World War with the potential to alter the course of history. When Peter told his dad about his plans to make *The Final Countdown*, Kirk told him to forget it. Peter planned somehow to borrow the actual USS *Nimitz* for the film. Kirk told him he was out of his head. Peter succeeded in convincing United Artists to spend ten million dollars on the production. Then, in a real coup, he talked the Pentagon into letting them film aboard the *Nimitz*.

Kirk originally had no intention of being a part of this hare-brained scheme of Peter's, but Peter talked even him into appearing in the film. Kirk said he'd play the secondary part of a 1940s politician who's picked up out of the Pacific by the *Nimitz* after a brush with the Japs. But as he studied the script and recognized the qualities in it, he settled on playing the starring role of the Captain of the *Nimitz*.

Even long after the film was made, Kirk remains truly impressed at the problems that Peter, then just twenty-three, was able to overcome. 'I couldn't believe that in his first film as a producer he got the navy's permission to use the aircraft carrier *Nimitz*, or that he even succeeded in getting someone to put up ten million dollars to make the film,' says a bemused but proud dad.

But despite Peter's success, Kirk was still worried, because Peter was starting at the top. It seemed all too easy. Kirk would have preferred his son to start at the bottom, climbing the rungs one at a time and getting involved with less ambitious projects along the way. Kirk admits to having mixed feelings about the whole thing. Although he has done his best to discourage his sons from going into movies, he confesses that inwardly he's proud that they have gone into the business, despite his warnings, and his warnings have been many.

> I've always told my sons that they haven't had the advantages I had because I was born poor. That is an advantage. You have nowhere to go but up. But when kids are born with a certain amount of affluence, they know they're going to have enough to eat. I went through a lot of periods where I didn't have enough to eat.
>
> And I think for kids who are not concerned about that, to still develop a drive and want to do something, want to function, is a much greater accomplishment than what I did. Because I *had* to try and do something. It was entirely up to me—to fight or become nothing.
>
> They didn't have that motivation. They could have copped out like a lot of other people. So, to me, the key word is *function*. All I want my sons to do is *something* in life.

The *something* they all chose was ultimately, and perhaps inevitably, movies. Even though Kirk spent most of his father-hood giving them the negatives of the business, telling them how many people wanted to be in the business and how so few succeeded. How it's filled with heartbreak and disappointment. Even Anne had become active in cautioning Peter and Eric as she evolved into a sort of 'boss of operations' from home, where she spent many hours debating with lawyers, making investments and creating production companies other than Bryna.

Kirk has always tried to let his sons stand on their own feet, without interfering in any way. To his surprise, though, all four seem to be succeeding. As Kirk himself says, 'I wasn't even going to be in Peter's film *The Final Countdown*, remember? *I'm* the one who said he couldn't do it! But then, too, look what happened when I handed *One Flew Over The Cuckoo's Nest* to Michael because *I* couldn't get it accepted.'

Despite the fact that the boys all shunned Kirk's advice, and the initial anger he felt when Eric went ahead and entered RADA without letting him know, Kirk remains immoveably proud as a father. 'And I'm proudest of all,' he says, 'that they seem to be functioning well within their chosen areas. All four of them. It makes me feel pretty good.'

NINETEEN/
/Who Says Kirk Douglas Can Ride An 'Orse?

Throughout his career Kirk Douglas had succeeded in upsetting people, but never before a
whole nation: in 1981 he was in trouble with the
whole of Australia. They resented the fact that he, an *American*,
was portraying one of their very own national folk heroes in the
Australian motion picture, *The Man From Snowy River*.

The film was based on a famous poem by A. B. 'Banjo'
Paterson, and told of a mountain boy's elevation to manhood in
the rugged and often treacherous setting of the Australian High
Country. Australian film producer Geoff Burrowes had offered
the script of *The Man From Snowy River* to Kirk several times.
Burrowes didn't want Kirk for the title role since that had to go
to a much younger man. In fact, Australian TV soap-opera star
Tom Burlinson landed that role. But Burrowes did have a
major part for Kirk. *Two* major roles in fact. He wanted Kirk to
portray twin brothers—one of them a smart, successful and
conniving landowner, the other a grizzled, kindly and humorous gold prospector.

Kirk had many misgivings: Australian films were generally
not successful internationally, although there had been excep-
tions, and he had never even heard of Geoff Burrowes or the
film's director, George Miller.

Each time Burrowes offered him the script, Kirk turned it down flat, so Burrowes urged him to read the poem. Intrigued, Kirk did and was captivated by it. The ability he had had as a boy to bring a poem to life had not been lost. He saw the whole story coming to life and he was suddenly struck by the challenge of playing twin brothers. He also saw his opportunity to make yet another unusual western, since *The Man From Snowy River* was to all intents and purposes an Australian western.

He accepted the part and took an eighteen-hour flight to Australia. He landed with quite a bump. The whole of the Australian press were there to welcome him by handing him a can of Australian beer, a bushman's hat and a whip.

''Old these, mate,' said one photographer, and as Kirk silently obliged the cameras virtually blinded him, so eager were the photographers to capture this picture on film. When they were satisfied, Kirk graciously handed back the borrowed equipment and took a seat, bracing himself for the onslaught of questions. The reporters' hostility was evident.

''Ow much are you getting paid for the film?'

'None of your damn business,' replied Kirk, and then added with good humour, 'but it's not enough anyway.'

As the interrogation continued, Kirk decided it was time to quell the hostility. He announced that he would recite the poem of 'The Man From Snowy River'. The place suddenly fell silent as he began to retell the great Australian legend which culminates in the climactic ride in which the young lad of the title out-paces all of the local horsemen in a race to head off a great black colt leading a pack of wild horses. Kirk had learned the whole poem by heart, but after a few moments he stopped, scratched his dimpled chin, and said, 'Let's see, how does the next line go?'

Kirk hadn't forgotten the lines. But he had a hunch that none of the newspapermen there even knew the poem. He waited for someone to give him the next line. No one did. He was right. They didn't know it. So he continued to captivate them with Paterson's words. When he finished he said to the pressmen, 'You really ought to read it, you know. It's beautiful.' After that, as one reporter noted, 'When Douglas stood up, he seemed to be a lot taller than when he had sat down.'

The reporters had been placated. But there was more hostility to come. Kirk next found himself being driven from Melbourne over a two-and-a-half-hour ride to the tiny outback town of Marrijig where the film was to be made and where Kirk would be spending the next several weeks. The town consisted of little more than one perpetually filled pub, a church and a handful of houses. The locals were not happy at having Kirk Douglas in their midst. It wasn't anything personal against him: they just didn't like an American playing an Australian. Each night they would gather in the pub and all heartily agree that Kirk Douglas should go home. It got so that Kirk was unable even to enjoy a drink in the one pub available.

'We got Australian actors as good as Kirk Douglas,' they'd say. 'Ya don't need to be a movie star to ride an 'orse. Who says Kirk Douglas can ride an 'orse, anyhow?' Kirk took all the criticism and the attempts to intimidate him in his stride. 'I like Australians,' he announced, 'because they're rude and impulsive, outspoken and direct—just like Americans!'

Although Kirk had not heard of the makers of this film, it did prove to be a prestigious production. It had the backing of 20th Century-Fox who were spending three million dollars on the picture. One million of that was Kirk's fee. The film also boasted Australian star Jack Thompson, who had shot to international fame with his acclaimed performance in *Breaker Morant*. Kirk knew that he had not fallen in among amateurs, then.

For the spectacular ride-out sequence ninety horses and forty men charged hell-for-leather in front of the cameras. The forty men were all experienced horsemen, but few could have boasted more experience with horses than Kirk Douglas who was an expert, having made so many westerns. Nevertheless, filming this sequence was an exhilarating and somewhat frightening experience for Kirk.

Explains co-producer Simon Wincer: 'During the shooting of the ride-out, Kirk was supposed to lead the riders in the charge. That wild-eyed look on his face, however, is only partly acting. George Miller, the director, told them all to "ride like hell" and Kirk knew that if he fell off, the boys would ride right over him.'

Although all those involved in making the film had the greatest respect and admiration for Kirk, the locals remained unimpressed. They continued to express their disgust. 'What everyone here has forgotten,' said Kirk in his own defence, 'is that a hundred years ago there were thousands of Americans in Australia looking for gold.' You should never underestimate Kirk Douglas. He is a stickler for research and authenticity. 'There's nobody more suited to play this part,' he proclaimed. 'Or *parts*. It just happens to be perfect casting.'

The Man From Snowy River turned out to be a superb film and the Australian nation quickly forgave Kirk when they saw his stunning performances. The picture quickly became the most successful Australian film of all time and proved to be a tremendous hit in the States.

Following *The Man From Snowy River* Kirk was due to make *First Blood* with Sylvester Stallone in Canada. But when Kirk arrived in Canada, he walked into another storm. When *First Blood* had first been offered to Kirk, he had turned it down. He was unimpressed with both the script and the original choice of director. He was promised that both the screenplay and the director would be changed, and upon that condition Kirk agreed to do the film. When he got to Canada he took one look at the script they handed him and he recognized it as the one they had first shown him and which he had turned down. He demanded to know what was going on.

'Stallone liked this version of the script,' he was told. 'He's got artistic control over this picture.'

Nobody had told Kirk about that. He announced he was catching the next plane back to California. The producers begged him to stay and said that he ought to talk it over with Stallone. Kirk agreed to stay and talk. The trouble was, according to Kirk, he waited a week and never even got to see Stallone. 'You really cannot expect me to do a screenplay which I'd already turned down,' he told the producers, and he left. It was the first time in his career that he had ever walked off a picture. As it turned out, *First Blood* proved to be a big, big hit for big, big Sly Stallone, competing with and sometimes even surpassing *ET* in box office receipts around the world.

Leaving the *First Blood* fiasco behind, Kirk was sent on yet another goodwill tour, this time to Red China. It proved to be a most peculiar experience for Kirk. The Chinese did not see American films and they had no idea who Kirk Douglas was. One day Kirk and Anne walked into Peking's Great Square, and there he froze for a few moments at the sight of a huge crowd. He expected them all suddenly to notice him and engulf him in a tide of adulation, but no one moved. No one batted an eye lid. He'd forgotten that nobody knew him—to them he was just another western tourist. It unnerved him at first, and then he took full advantage of being able to walk abroad in complete anonymity.

He wasn't unknown by all in China, however. There were plenty of foreign diplomats from around the world who knew of Kirk Douglas the Hollywood star. When the American Ambassador threw a reception in honour of Kirk, the turnout was astounding, to the amazement of the Ambassador. He knew that most diplomats found these receptions for visiting ambassadors a bore and were usually unenthusiastic about attending them. But everyone seemed to be there.

When Kirk learned of the American Ambassador's surprise, the movie star said, 'It's proved what I've always known. A lot more people are interested in movies than in politics.'

TWENTY/
Follow Your Own
Instinct

For eighteen years Kirk had happily allowed his work to be constantly interrupted so that he could faithfully fulfil his obligations to the United States and the American Government by visiting whatever countries they asked him to. In 1981 his country rewarded him for all his loyal efforts when the White House gave him the well-deserved Medal of Freedom, the highest civilian award. It was for his 'significant cultural endeavors as an actor and a goodwill ambassador'.

It was one of Kirk's proudest moments when he received the award. It meant more to him than any of the Oscars which had eluded him throughout his career. It satisfied him to know that the debt he always felt he owed his country for allowing him to have the education to launch him in his career was considered paid in full. But he didn't stop his touring on behalf of the Information Agency. He continues to spread goodwill around the globe, and in 1983 he received a second award from the White House: in the United States Supreme Court Chambers in Washington, he was given the Jefferson Award 'for greatest public service performed by a private citizen'. In that same year he received the Albert Einstein Award from Israel's Institute of Technology. These awards and medals are much prized and hang in special places in his Beverly Hills home among the works of art and autographed pictures of past American Presidents.

Born in 1916, in the 1980s Kirk Douglas has few ambitions left except to keep on working. And that he does with a vigour and an undying enthusiasm which has marked his whole career.

In 1981 he partially fulfilled one remaining ambition, which was to appear in a play on the London stage with Burt Lancaster. It happened, but he had to be content with a stage in San Francisco. The play was *The Boys Of Autumn*, the story of Tom Sawyer and Huckleberry Finn in their twilight years. It was an odd play, written by a Chicago college professor, Bernard Sabath, in which the two old friends just happen to meet on a hill overlooking the Mississippi. At first they don't recognize each other, but when they do they sit down together and talk about their lives. They both confess to startling crimes. Lancaster as Huck admits to the mercy killing of his wife, while Douglas as Tom makes the pathetic admission of child molesting.

The play was hard-going for the two ageing men, particularly for Lancaster who just a year or so later would undergo emergency heart surgery. Rehearsals took up twelve hours every day. One day Kirk said to Burt, 'Aren't we too rich for all this?'

The whole experience was a tough but gratifying one for both men. Their friendship grew ever more warmer, and they enjoyed an immensely successful run with the play. It drew in the crowds, not because of the play itself, but because of the appearances of Kirk Douglas and Burt Lancaster. Neither man felt that the play was as good as it should have been, and they found it far too exhausting to continue with it. They agreed to call it a day and return to film making, which they found a much easier medium to exhibit their talents in.

Determined not to allow age to force him into character acting, Kirk continues to pick and choose his film roles, and in the past few years has appeared in very different roles. In *Home Movies*, he was the patriarch of a mad family whose zany antics compared favourably with those in the TV sit-com *Soap*. In the film Kirk's family find that suicide, revenge and promiscuity are everyday occurrences.

He next picked a subject he felt strongly about. He played the survivor of a Nazi concentration camp in *Remembrance Of Love*, a tearjerker in which he goes back to Israel with his daughter, played by Pam (*Mork And Mindy*) Dawber to discover the fate of the woman he loved.

In 1983 he made a religious drama called *The Shadow Of God*, which was filmed in and around the Vatican. In 1984 he finally got to make the western he had long dreamed of filming, *Draw!*, but Burt Lancaster wasn't available to whoop it up with him in this fun film. Instead, he had James Coburn co-starring.

Draw! represents the latest display of Kirk's businessman's nature. Over the past few years there has been a change within the industry brought about by video and cable vision. In fact, both *Home Movies* and *Remembrance Of Love*, like so many films of recent years which didn't feature laser guns or swords and sorcery, found their audiences among the video enthusiasts before either film had a chance to play a decent cinema release. This, and the potential in America's ever-growing cable television stations, prompted Kirk to take another official stab at producing and make *Draw!* specifically for cable television in the States and cinemas in all other countries.

He remains as optimistic as ever about his film, and about the future. He says:

> I think it's an exciting period. I think sometimes studio heads are kind of a little upset. They don't know how to deal with what's happening with pay-cable television. Those of us who are actors or producers see it as another avenue, another channel, to show our wares. So it's exciting.
>
> You have many more people involved in making movies. Now, most movies are independent productions. It's not like when I first came here and the studios controlled the making of all the movies. Now it's a bunch of usually young people getting together, developing a script and casting it and making the film.
>
> So it's exciting, and to be a part of the excitement is to identify yourself with this wave of youth. And with four sons of varying ages, I have the advantage of being in close proximity with that wave.

Certainly with the exception of Kirk and Jim Coburn, the rest of the cast and crew of *Draw!* are young people. But still Kirk insists on doing as much of the action as he is able to, and that's still a considerable amount.

Despite his enthusiasm and motivation in making *Draw!* specifically for cable television, he is likely to raise his voice when someone tries to make a distinction between films for TV and films for the cinema. 'I don't understand it,' he says, 'when they say a TV-movie or a theatrical movie. They're either good movies or bad movies.' And he has a good argument for those who would claim that westerns are out of date. 'They never went out,' he says. 'Black hats became Darth Vader and .44 bullets became laser beams.'

So Kirk Douglas goes on making movies, making westerns. He also continues to enjoy close family ties with his four boys and especially with wife Anne who, he says, is still his best friend.

He doesn't forget his background or his mama who is dead now. He doesn't forget his father either, though his memories of Herschel are always tinged with bitterness. Life for Issur Danielovitch has been one long lesson: learning how to fight, how to grow, how to give back what you owe, how to be a child, how to be a parent, how to go with the tide—how to be an individual.

No doubt he'll always be best remembered for being a sonofabitch. He'll also be remembered for being a superior actor. Film buffs will certainly remember him for being an independent and courageous producer. A few like James Stacy will remember him for his generosity. His government will remember him for his patriotism and his loyalty.

He may still achieve something that will outshine all his previous achievements, because if there's one thing you can count on Kirk Douglas to do, it's the unexpected. He's certainly not through with films, not by a long shot. And he'll continue to follow his own instincts to ensure he can keep on making films.

'I've made good films, bad films, had successes and failures, but I have never made a film that the studio lost money with,' he claims. 'There is no secret about it; you have to become your own critic and set a standard for yourself. There is no magical way.

'Follow your own instinct and hope that you are right.'

175

TWENTY-ONE / The Russian Drive

'**9** want all my sons to surpass me,' Kirk Douglas has said. 'That is a form of immortality.'

One would think that Kirk has already ensured his immortality through his own achievements. But then, Kirk has never been a man to sit back and rest on past laurels. Which is why he's still going strong.

However, it must have seemed to him for a while that his days as a movie star were numbered. His 1983 picture *Remembrance of Love*, like *Home Movies* two years before that, hardly saw the light of day, except on video. And even as video releases, neither film could ever hope to compete in a rental and purchase market which is dominated by films like *Rambo*, *Indiana Jones* and youth-oriented comedies.

The Shadow of God seems to have disappeared without a trace, and only *Draw!* found an audience on cable TV. Kirk's hope that it would be released theatrically outside of his own country faded into the movie-western sunset as one of a series of attempts to resurrect the Western genre which bit the dust. Clint Eastwood came close to success in riding the range once again in *Pale Rider*, but just about every other horse opera since the disastrous *Heaven's Gate* in 1980 has proven box office poison.

Kirk did have one of his dreams materialize, though (although one suspects that somewhere along the line it may have hurt a little bit), because he has undoubtedly been surpassed by one of his sons, Michael. Not that anyone could claim yet that Michael has surpassed his father in terms of movie history—

though that may yet happen. But it's certainly true in terms of movies today.

Since 1984 Kirk has had to take a back seat while Michael went from strength to strength as both a producer and actor. It has become impossible to write about the Kirk Douglas story without detailing the rise of his oldest son to the point where Kirk recently told Michael, 'Being your father is getting to be a pain in the ass!'

Says Michael, 'Now he knows what it was like when I was growing up and he was getting so much attention.'

But Kirk isn't slow to let his first-born know how proud he is of the way Michael's handled his success. Kirk always wanted the best for his four sons, but he expected them to work for it. Undoubtedly, Michael had the advantage of being the oldest of his sons because he was the first to emerge in movies bearing the Douglas name— although at times it was also a distinct disadvantage. 'Everyone expected me to be the son of *Spartacus*,' says Michael. 'I used to think, How can I ever be the man my father is? That's why I've turned down acting parts similar to his—to prevent comparisons.'

Kirk has never interfered with his sons' careers—except for doing his best to dissuade them from following in his footsteps, a task in which he failed totally. But he hasn't tried to help them, either. Everything his sons have wanted to achieve had to be done on their own.

But in other areas of their lives, Kirk is always ready to step in with a fatherly word or two of advice. Sometimes, though, he has been too fatherly, reigning over the Douglas family in true patriarchal style. His second oldest son, Joel, found it necessary to move away from the family environment to pursue his career as a successful TV producer and sometimes film producer.

He says:

> Dad is the all-powerful one in the family. It's hard to be an individual when he's about. That's why I moved to New York to work when I was younger. He's intense to the point that you feel he will eat you up. I suppose that's what made him a big star for so long.

Joel, of all the sons, is perhaps the one least likely to succeed in coping with his father's well-meant nagging. ('I nag my sons because I care about them,' says Kirk.) Joel is by all accounts the 'softie' of the clan and, according to his stepmother, 'the nicest member of the family—a teddy bear who falls in love every other month.'

His sensitivity resulted in years of suffering terrible nightmares as a boy when he saw his father cut off an ear in *Lust For Life*.

Joel remains close to his father and the rest of the family, in particular to Michael, with whom he has often worked in partnership. But Kirk has never been one to spare the rod to spoil the boys.

'Dad was very strict,' says Michael. 'We used to fight all the time, but it was only because he cared. When Joel and I were just boys, he could have easily just given us our allowance every week and then said, "Goodbye."'

But Kirk has never been a father to stand back and watch silently whenever one of his boys has gone through a bleak period in their personal lives. In 1984 he saw his oldest son falling into a typical Hollywood trap that threatened his marriage—and having already been there himself, Kirk didn't want to see Michael go through the agonies of a divorce.

It began with a four-and-a-half year obsession of Michael's to bring *Romancing The Stone* to the screen. Originally, he intended only to produce it and was looking for a star name to play the lead role of Jack Colton. When a friend read the screenplay, it was suggested to Michael that this was a part *he* should play.

'I thought about it,' said Michael, 'and realized that of all the characters I've played, this one was closest to the real me.'

His total involvement with the project over a long period of time meant that his marriage to wife Diandra took a back seat in his life.

For Diandra the whole experience of getting married, giving up her own promising career and moving to California was traumatic enough, but now as she saw Michael becoming increasingly involved in his own work, she felt like she was being lost in his shadow, even as Michael was once lost in his father's.

It was Kirk who, by all accounts, saw this pattern emerging and encouraged Michael to seriously consider the consequences of totally immersing himself in work. Kirk himself has always been a workaholic, but there can be no denying that since his second marriage, he has done all he could to make it work and to be a good father.

But by the time Kirk had stepped in, much of the damage had been done, and Michael and Diandra agreed to a trial separation.

Since Michael was to go to Mexico to film *Romancing The Stone*, it seemed the ideal time for him and his wife to be apart. It was a rough time for all concerned, not least of all for Michael—who not only had to consider how he was going to save his marriage, but who also had to bear the burden as actor and producer on possibly the toughest film he'll ever make.

The production was fraught with problems—not the least of which was the weather. The Mexican location was constantly awash with eight inches of rain. Heavy filming equipment was continually getting bogged down, and rivers were forever bursting their banks.

He and leading lady Kathleen Turner suffered such indignities as being hauled through mud and rocks, and actors and crew were frequently meeting with accidents. The worst moment occurred when a crocodile grabbed the animal trainer's hand in its powerful jaws. Frantic efforts were made to pry the beast's mouth open with paddles and boards until the trainer was free. He'd lost a lot of blood and only just kept his hand intact when the Rolex watch he was wearing prevented the croc from totally severing his hand at the wrist.

By the time Michael returned to Hollywood he had decided what to do to save his marriage. He moved his family out of Hollywood and into New York, where they still live in an eight-room apartment overlooking Central Park. Here they sought out new friends and new interests away from the world of movie-making. Michael had also made up his mind to spend his time between films with his wife and son, and to make their time together worthwhile. To help him in this, he bought a country holiday home where the family could escape city life and enjoy nobody else's company but their own.

Much of it was a compromise because, says Michael:

I can't balance my responsibility as a father and a husband with my work. My work comes first. But when the job is done, my family is my priority.

The problem was, because I like my work too much, I didn't give enough time to my family. Actors are paid to be selfish and self-involved. You have to admit your insecurities to someone, and I do to Diandra. The problem is that when you are producing you cannot admit your insecurities to anyone—even yourself.

179

It must have been the memories of his own childhood, when his mother and father divorced, which helped to bring Michael to his senses. He could remember flying from east to west and back again, from mother to father, and on every journey his younger brother Joel would cry.

And besides his concern for Cameron, Michael had realized he still loved Diandra.

The success of *Romancing The Stone* prompted a sequel, *The Jewel Of The Nile*, filmed in Morocco. This time Diandra and Cameron accompanied him whenever and wherever it was possible. As a child, Michael spent many happy times on location with his dad, and he knew how important it was for his own son to be as close to him as possible while he was working.

> Cameron would get up very early each morning and come on the set with me, finding different things to entertain and amuse himself all day. It was just great having him there with me and kind of reminded me of when I was his age [seven] visiting my father on his movies.

But there is much more to Michael's character than simple experience that comes from Kirk. 'My father is of Russian heritage,' says Michael, 'and it's the Russian part of me that gives me drive.'

It's that drive that has resulted in Michael's ongoing success, which continued with *The Jewel Of The Nile*. Michael claims it has also resulted in a certain amount of aggressiveness. This is very much a part of Kirk's make-up, but with Michael it is less intense and seldom noticed by others.

'I can be aggressive,' says Michael. 'I can be pretty intense and I have inherited some of that from my father, although I think he had a rougher edge to his aggression.'

Despite this, Michael has become one of the most popular people in Hollywood. (What a contrast to his father who was once dubbed 'The Most Hated Man In Hollywood.') He always makes a point of being polite to people but, he claims, he often feels like behaving differently.

He says it's because he feels a responsibility to his family. 'That's one of the dilemmas of being second generation. My father is an international star who is appreciated and well-respected. I don't want to let him down, so sometimes when you feel like not being polite you have to because you're in the same business.'

Kirk confirms Michael's claim to be less than the nice guy everyone thinks he is. Says Kirk:

> I just don't believe Michael is as sweet and charming as everyone says. Oh, he's tough! There's a piece of steel inside of him. I tell you, if I were cornered in a saloon with my back against the wall, Michael's the guy I would want beside me.

Nevertheless, I find it hard to believe that Michael isn't perhaps being self-defamatory in saying he is only reluctantly polite. Not long ago I met a struggling actor from America who, to earn the money he wasn't making in acting, was waiting on tables in a restaurant. One of his customers one day happened to be Michael Douglas.

The waiter didn't intend to impose on Michael but told him that he was also an actor. Michael then took time to talk to the waiter, listening to his problems and offering advice, and wished him good luck.

I also have some first-hand experience of his consideration, as well as a little of Kirk's own brand of generosity. The first time I met Kirk in 1975, when he was in London to promote *Posse*, we discovered we had a common ground in our love of westerns. I told him I'd had a go at writing some western screenplays and he didn't hesitate in offering to read them for me. I didn't ask him. he actually offered. To ensure their safe arrival in Hollywood, he arranged for the film company that was releasing *Posse* to send the scripts—three in all—directly to him.

That was basically where his generosity stopped. I never heard back from him, no matter how many letters I wrote, having obtained his private address from the film company; and to the best of my knowledge he still has my scripts.

When Michael came to London to promote *One Flew Over The Cuckoo's Nest* I had the audacity to write to him at the Dorchester Hotel and tell him of my dilemma. A couple of weeks later he personally wrote to me, saying,

> I have just returned to Los Angeles and will immediately talk to my father about a response to your western scripts. Hopefully you will hear from him soon.
>
> Respectfully,
> Michael Douglas

P.S. I enjoyed your interview on my father and *Cuckoo's Nest*—well done!

I don't believe he had to do that, and I have no doubt he did talk to Kirk. (Unfortunately, I still didn't hear from Kirk, and when Kirk came to London recently for a press conference, I didn't have the courage to bring the subject up!)

I have since drawn my own conclusion that Kirk Douglas basically does whatever is good for Kirk Douglas. (God knows my scripts probably weren't good for anyone!) It's a formula of his that you can't really knock although maybe it goes some way to explaining why he's made enemies along the way to success. Mind you, as Michael says, today Kirk is appreciated and well respected. But then he is a survivor, and one of the great names of Hollywood. He has achieved what he set out to do, but even that isn't enough. Not for him. Not only does he plan to continue for as long as he can (and, judging by his amazing physique, that'll be for a long time to come), he now seems content to allow his sons to go all-out for success to equal his—having once done all he could to stop them. Even his grandson Cameron seems destined for greatness—if Granddad has anything to do with it.

'I've got them all out working,' jokes Kirk. 'The only one who is still doing nothing is my grandson Cameron. I don't understand it. He seems to think he can get away with it just because he's got a dimple on his chin!'

TWENTY-TWO

"Tough Guy"

On 1987 everybody was talking about *Fatal Attraction*, the huge box office success starring Michael Douglas. Despite the fact that it was about the violent consequences of an extramarital affair, the publicity and press coverage concentrated on the lusty content of the film and hailed Michael as 'the sexiest man on screen.'

That's no mean feat for a man well into his forties, competing with today's younger screen stars like Tom Cruise or Michael J. Fox—especially when, in between films as Michael is first to admit, he tends to go to seed. But on screen he looks like a man ten years younger. While shooting *Fatal Attraction* he was 43, exactly the same age as his father was at the pinnacle of his career when he made *Spartacus*. Back in those late fifties and early sixties it was the Epic Film that attracted millions to the cinema. Today Hollywood gets people to leave their homes and head for the local movie house with star-studded, almost sexually explicit films—films that have something to offer beyond a few scenes of stimulating action, films such as *Body Heat* and the remake of *The Postman Always Rings Twice*.

'I've always wanted to make a film about pure lust,' says Michael, but in his case he wanted to put an original slant on things. 'If we're really honest with each other,' he says, 'maybe more than once there's been a woman in the office or at a party that you just want to go to bed with. You don't know them and they may not even be beautiful. It's a chemical thing, an animal thing. Everyone has been in those situations. Most of the time they don't act on them, but sometimes they do. It's a thing that interests me.'

There seem to be a lot of women around who would claim that Michael himself has fallen into this trap, but he denies it emphatically.

'Woman have confronted Diandra saying "I'm having an affair with Michael," or "I spent the night with him." These are women I've never even met. I don't even know their names.

'That's been the case since I became some sort of a celebrity.'

Diandra accepts these moments as being an occupational hazard of having a movie star for a husband. 'You just take it with a grain of salt,' she says, and then adds, 'two grains of salt.'

She wasn't even upset at seeing her husband getting his clothes ripped off by Glenn Close and then engage in some of the hottest scenes Hollywood has dared to film.

On the way to the premiere of *Fatal Attraction* Michael said to Diandra, 'Honey, there are a couple of scenes which I don't want you to get too upset about.'

He says, 'She got so involved in the film that the hot scenes came and went without her thinking to stop and say "Hey! What were you doing there?"'

So where does all this leave Kirk, thirty years older than Michael and himself once considered one of the sexiest men in movies?

In the opinion of Peter Douglas, his dad is still a sex symbol. 'I get very jealous of him being so sexy,' says Peter. 'I can see how women are turned on by him. Women still come up to him and ask to touch his dimple. Dad just laughs it off. I think he handles it very well.'

For years Anne Douglas has been aware of Kirk's sexual magnetism. Like Diandra, she has had to deal with the fact that she's married to a man that a great many women would like to get between the sheets with. He's always been attractive to women, even as a student at the American Academy of Dramatic Arts in New York where a young girl, Diana Dill, told an even younger Lauren Bacall, 'Don't ever get mixed up with anyone like Kirk. You'll get hurt because actors are unreliable and not to be trusted. Have some fun with him, but don't get serious.'

The fact was that Lauren Bacall was madly in love with the young Kirk Douglas and had visions of marrying him. Instead, it was Diana Dill who married him.

His second wife, Anne, grew used to having women trying to throw themselves at her husband and has said, 'Either I was going to be in a constant state of trauma or I had to ignore it.'

The marriage between Kirk and Anne is as strong as ever. She has had to work as hard as he has to make it work.

'I give as much as I can to my husband,' she says. 'He gets more than anybody else and comes first in my life. Actors and performers need a lot of attention.'

As for Kirk's career, the mid-eighties were beginning to look as lean as his own incredible physique. Not even he would argue the point that it has been Michael who has kept the Douglas flag flying over the past few years, during which Kirk has been noticeably less active. But maybe that's not such a bad thing for someone who deserves a break now and again.

Michael has noted:

I've seen from my father's career that he'd never had the chance to enjoy his success. I mean, he's made seventy-odd films and I know that he wishes he'd had the chance to take a little time out here and there. But that's the way it was in those days.

The trouble is, Kirk can't sit still for ever. He's always looking for the kind of picture *he'd* like to make.

'If I like a picture I do it. I don't stop to wonder if it will be successful or not. Some of the pictures I'm most proud of—*Lonely Are The Brave* and *Paths of Glory*—did not make a lot of money. But I'm very glad I made them.'

Most of the scripts he gets sent (probably like mine) are not worth a second glance, but when one did come along called *Tough Guys* in 1986, with roles tailor-made for him and his old sparring partner Burt Lancaster, he jumped for it.

It told the story of two once-notorious criminals who are released from prison after a 35-year sentence to discover a whole new world that they've never known and which has long forgotten them. To remind everyone of who they are—or once were—they plan a spectacular train robbery the likes of which America—or anywhere else, for that matter—have not seen in years.

It was filmed at the Disney studios for Touchstone Films (a sort of adult subsidiary of Disney) where, from the set, Burt Lancaster said:

In a way it's a spoof of both our careers, Kirk's and mine. These two swashbuckling bandits are so disturbed by what they find, especially the lack of chivalry, that they go back to carrying out robberies *their* way. I really think it's going to be a delightful film.

And it was. They could never boast that it was the best film they'd ever made, but it set out to entertain, with these two legends keeping their tongues firmly implanted in their cheeks. For both stars it proved that they could still compete with the best of today's crop of young actors. It had something of the so-called 'street movie' style about it, but there's no doubting that Kirk and Burt made sure they did it their way.

It is hard to believe that Kirk was then seventy and Burt three years older. Not that anyone should challenge Kirk on his age because he can boast, 'I can still do everything I used to do thirty years ago—only I don't do it as often!'

During filming, the old camaraderie was still there, and each star took delight in sending himself up. 'Burt plays golf and I play tennis,' said Kirk. 'I told him that when I get to be an old man, I'll take up *his* game.'

Actually, Kirk used to play golf but gave it up about ten years ago, along with smoking, to play tennis. He says he gave up golf because he got stuck for hours playing with people who bored him. 'If you don't like the people you're playing with, when you play tennis,'' he points out, 'you can be aggressive.'

Whether or not he really believes it, Kirk refuses to admit that he is well past his prime. 'Someone asked me the other day what it felt like to be old,' he said. 'I told them to come back in thirty years and then I might be able to tell them.'

He's not afraid to show everyone how lean and fit he is either. In fact, there has to be something of the exhibitionist in him. In one scene in *Tough Guys*, when the two stars are pursued aboard a train, Kirk drops his trousers to reveal his bare behind. He must be the oldest mooner in movie history. In fact, not only his bare *derrièr* was in full view of the camera in a scene from *Saturn 3*, but just about all of him. Only a carefully angled camera prevented a nude Kirk Douglas from being seen totally full frontal. Even back in 1967 Kirk did a shot in *The War Wagon* which showed his posterior, but that was cut by the studio who thought it was too much bare cheek for its time.

Kirk is quick to take credit for the mooning sequence in *Tough Guys*.

186

That was my idea. All the best ideas in the films I make come from me.

When my sons were in college they used to drive by in their cars and moon at people. So I thought, here's this old guy in the film giving the finger to everyone, so why not do some mooning as well?

On the subject of his long-term partnership with Lancaster, Kirk says, 'Burt and I were always considered the most difficult actors in Hollywood. Well, I don't think we were difficult. We were just professionals.'

His admiration for Burt is still glowing. In comparing him to another frequent screen partner, John Wayne, Kirk said:

John Wayne was a great *star*. But he always played Wayne. Anthing else he didn't regard as manly.

Now someone like Burt Lancaster is just the opposite. The living proof that you can be a sensitive actor and macho at the same time.

Following their previous partnership in the play *The Boys Of Autumn*, Burt and Kirk really didn't expect to have the opportunity to work together again. Then along came *Tough Guys* which, when released in 1987, not only rekindled their respect and admiration for each other, but undoubtedly revitalised Kirk's career.

'Burt and I originally thought we might make this our last film,' said Kirk, 'as a kind of homage to ourselves. But now I've got other projects coming up, and we might make a sequel.'

Following *Tough Guys* Kirk worked on a mini-series, *Queenie*, which captured a huge audience on American television in 1987. It was based on the life of movie legend Merle Oberon and starred, in the title role, 19-year-old up-and-coming actress Mia Sara. It was filmed in various parts of the world, including India and London, and featured a love-making scene between the young actress and seventy-year-old Kirk. It was not, of course, anywhere near as hot as the scenes Michael did with Glenn Close in *Fatal Attraction*, but Anne Douglas was not slow to point out to her husband that in *Tough Guys* he made love to a 26-year-old and then in *Queenie* he made love to an even younger 19-year-old woman. 'You'd better watch your step,' she told him, 'or you'll be accused of child molesting!'

'I don't mind one bit,' replied Kirk. 'I'll keep on going until they arrest me!'

It was during 1987 that he came to London for a press conference to promote *Tough Guys*. At the hotel where he held court, he demonstrated his agility by removing his jacket and performing a few acrobatics on the sofa, to the delight of the gaggle of photographers. 'Old age is a point of view,' he told everyone. 'You've gotta take care of your body, of course.'

When some skeptic asked him if it was really his bare behind displayed in *Tough Guys* or a stand-in's, he was quick to retort, 'No, no, that was *me*.'

While Kirk was enjoying himself immensely with two successes in a row, Michael was back in New York working on a picture called *Wall Street*. Working in what was now his home town, as he also did with *Fatal Attraction*, he was able to go home each night to his family, strengthening all his efforts to keep the marriage alive and the family a complete unit. It seems very likely that this is something he may continue to do when producing movies— helping to balance the roles of family man and film producer more evenly than a few years back.

The film was a complete departure from his usual heroic image, portraying a ruthless, odious, greedy Wall Street inside trader. It was a chilling, thoroughly believable performance that earned him an Oscar nomination.

As the 1988 Academy Awards ceremony approached, the whole Douglas family made plans to meet afterward for a celebration, whether he won or not. It turned out to be something to really celebrate when Michael was awarded with the little golden statue by the American Academy. Once again Michael had succeeded in an area where Kirk has failed. Winning an Oscar as Best Actor was a dream that has still eluded Kirk, but there was no doubting the pride and emotion he felt at his son's triumph. Michael's acceptance speech was extremely moving when he thanked his father for allowing his son to step out of his shadow.

Upon hearing the news that Michael had won his Oscar, a proud, emotional father telephoned and said, 'I hope you won't mind, but I don't think I ought to come to the celebration tonight. It wouldn't look good for my macho image if I were seen crying in public.' So Kirk stayed at home to celebrate Michael's victory quietly with Anne.

He has said that he wanted his sons to surpass him, and Michael is the one who has managed to do that. When asked recently how his father felt about his Oscar, Michael said he believed that for Kirk it meant not only pride in a son's achievements, but also something more to add to his immortality.

His other sons may also yet achieve greater things. Peter, Anne's oldest son by Kirk, continues to produce movies but seems to have no intention of taking up acting. However, this is the son Kirk seems to feel more of an affinity with, and says, 'Of all my sons, Peter is the one who is most like me. He's volatile, impatient, and,' he adds with a twinkle in those ever-alert eyes, 'extremely bright!'

The one big difference between Peter and Kirk is that, unlike Peter, Kirk still spends money sparingly as a direct result of his poor upbringing, as though having attained so much wealth he can never take it all for granted. But Peter *does* take it all for granted.

'Once I really had to nag Dad to change his battered old car,' he recalls. 'I'm not like my father as far as money is concerned. I grew up in comfort and I do like going first class.'

It's an attitude Kirk doesn't really argue with. 'Who knows?' he said at his press conference in London. 'If I'd had a rich father like Kirk Douglas, I might have ended up playing polo.'

The least known and least successful so far of all his sons is Eric, the youngest. And being the youngest he's probably had it tougher than the others, as most do when they are the last-born. He was the son Kirk had hoped would not go into movies. But having chosen to become an actor, and having even studied at RADA, not even the name Douglas has opened doors for him. He says, 'Producers prefer the non-acting Brat Pack,' and not even his brothers in their capacity as producers have chosen to make things easier for him. They have all gone out and made it on their own and Eric, it seems, must do the same. If not for the sake of his older brothers, then for Dad's sake.

As Michael says, 'Dad loves us, but you must earn his respect.'

But Eric isn't despondent. He promises, 'I'll be famous—one day.'

Unfortunately for him, as an actor he no longer has only his father's shadow hanging over him but Michael's, too.

Kirk is sympathetic to his sons' problems in dealing with having a famous father and how, for them, the almost unreal world they were brought up in made it all seem so easy to become just as rich and famous as Dad.

Says Kirk:

> My boys would turn on the television and watch their father killing a handful of Romans, and then they'd look around the room and see Tony Curtis sitting here and Burt Lancaster over there and maybe Gregory Peck coming through the door.
>
> That was a disadvantage they had to be helped to overcome. They had to be helped to know what was reality and to understand that for me this was just a way I made my living. Just like other fathers work in offices or factories. It's an obstacle all show-business kids have to overcome. Sometimes I'm amazed how well they have all dealt with it.

He still can't help reminding them from time to time just how tough it was for him. If he ever writes his autobiography, it will be for his sons.

'I've always wanted to write my life story,' he has said. 'I guess everyone does. But I could never think of a reason for writing it. Then I realised that... when I talk to my sons, there's so much they don't know about me.'

It's more than likely that they do know everything about him. He never stops telling them. But Kirk, perhaps, has never quite gotten over the fact that he came from nowhere and, with a little luck, a lot of love from his mother, and all the drive he could muster, he made it to the top.

For some, quitting while you're ahead is the best way to complete a dazzling career. But Kirk still has projects he hopes to fulfill and still expects to make at least one more movie with his pal Burt Lancaster.

However, he does allow himself one proviso when any mention of retirement is made. At his *Tough Guys* press conference in London he said, 'When I was making the film, my driver said to me, "Why does a very rich man like you work so hard?"

'I said that I enjoyed what I was doing. However, if someday the public says "No, Kirk, we don't want you anymore..."'

I can't help but think that if that day ever came, there's no way Kirk would give in graciously—not without a fight. He's been fighting all his life and there is nothing about him, even at the age of seventy-two, to suggest he would stop now. He is still one hell of a tough guy.

190

Filmography

1946

The Strange Love Of Martha Ivers. A Hal B. Wallis Production, distributed by Paramount. Directed by Lewis Milestone. Screenplay by Robert Rossen, based on a story by Jack Patrick. Cast: Barbara Stanwyck, Van Heflin, Lizabeth Scott, Kirk Douglas, Judith Anderson, Roman Bohnen.

1947

Out Of The Past. An RKO Picture. Produced by Warren Duff. Directed by Jacques Tourneur. Screenplay by Geoffrey Homes. Cast: Robert Mitchum, Jane Greer, Kirk Douglas, Rhonda Fleming, Richard Webb, Steve Brodie.

Mourning Becomes Electra. An RKO Picture. Produced, directed and written by Dudley Nichols. Based on the play by Eugene O'Neill. Cast: Rosalind Russell, Michael Redgrave, Raymond Massey, Katina Paxinou, Leon Genn, Kirk Douglas, Nancy Coleman.

I Walk Alone. A Hal B. Wallis Production, distributed by Paramount. Directed by Byron Haskins. Written by Charles Schnee. Based on the play *Beggars Are Coming To Town* by Theodore Reeves. Cast: Burt Lancaster, Lizabeth Scott, Kirk Douglas, Wendell Corey, Kristine Miller, George Riguard.

1948

The Walls Of Jericho. 20th Century-Fox. Produced by Lamar Trotti. Directed by John M. Stahl. Screenplay by Lamar Trotti from the novel by Paul Wellman. Cast: Cornel Wilde, Linda Darnell, Anne Baxter, Kirk Douglas, Anne Dvorak, Marjorie Rambeau.

My Dear Secretary. A Harry M. Popkin-Leo C. Popkin Production. Distributed by United Artists. Directed and written by Charles Martin. Cast: Laraine Day, Kirk Douglas, Keenan Wynn, Helen Walker, Rudy Vallee, Florence Bates.

A Letter To Three Wives. 20th Century-Fox. Produced by Sol C. Siegel. Directed and written by Joseph L. Mankiewicz from the novel by John Klempner. Cast: Jeanne Crain, Linda Darnell, Ann Southern, Kirk Douglas, Paul Douglas, Barbara Lawrence.

1949
Champion. A Screen Plays Production, distributed by United Artists. Produced by Stanley Kramer. Directed by Mark Robson. Written by Carl Foreman from a story by Ring Lardner. Cast: Kirk Douglas, Marilyn Maxwell, Arthur Kennedy, Paul Stewart, Ruth Roman, Lola Albright.

1950
Young Man With A Horn. Warner Bros. Produced by Jerry Wald. Directed by Michael Curtiz. Screenplay by Carl Foreman and Edmund H. North from the novel by Dorothy Baker. Cast: Kirk Douglas, Lauren Bacall, Doris Day, Hoagy Carmichael, Juano Hernandez, Jerome Cowan.

The Glass Menagerie. Warner Bros. Produced by Jerry Wald and Charles K. Feldman. Directed by Irving Rapper. Screenplay by Tennessee Williams and Peter Bernaise based on the play by Williams. Cast: Jane Wyman, Kirk Douglas, Gertrude Lawrence, Arthur Kennedy, Ralph Sanford, Ann Tyrell.

1951
Ace In The Hole (also known as *The Big Carnival*). Paramount. Produced and directed by Billy Wilder. Written by Wilder, Lesser Samuels and Walter Newman. Cast: Kirk Douglas, Jan Sterling, Bob Arthur, Porter Hall, Frank Cady, Richard Benedict.

Along The Great Divide. Warner Bros. Produced by Anthony Veiller. Directed by Raoul Walsh. Screenplay by Walter Doniger and Lewis Meltzer. Cast: Kirk Douglas, Virginia Mayo, John Agar, Walter Brennan, Ray Teal, Hugh Sanders.

Detective Story. Paramount. Produced and directed by William Wyler. Screenplay by Philip Yordon and Robert Wyler from the play by Sidney Kingsley. Cast: Kirk Douglas, Eleanor Parker, William Bendix, Lee Grant, Bert Freed, Frank Faylen.

1952
The Big Trees. Warner Bros. Produced by Louis F. Eledman. Directed by Felix Feist. Screenplay by John Twist and James R. Webb. Cast: Kirk Douglas, Eve Miller, Patrice Wymore, Edgar Buchanan, John Archer, Alan Hale, Jr.

The Big Sky. A Winchester Pictures Production, distributed by RKO Radio. Produced and directed by Howard Hawks. Screenplay by Dudley Nichols from the novel by A. B. Guthrie, Jr. Cast: Kirk Douglas, Dewey Martin, Elizabeth Threatt, Arthur Hunnicut, Buddy Baer, Steven Geray, Hank Worden, Jim Davis.

The Bad And The Beautiful. MGM. Produced by John Houseman. Directed by Vincente Minnelli. Screenplay by Charles Schnee. Cast: Lana Turner, Kirk Douglas, Walter Pidgeon, Dick Powell, Barry Sullivan, Gloria Grahame, Gilbert Roland, Leo G. Carroll.

1953
The Story Of Three Loves. MGM. Produced by Sidney Franklin. 'Equilibrium' was the last of three episodes, directed by Gottfried Reinhardt. Screenplay by John Collier. Cast: Pier Angeli, Kirk Douglas, Richard Anderson.

The Juggler. A Stanley Kramer Company Production, distributed by Columbia Pictures. Directed by Edward Dmytryk. Screenplay by Michael Blankfort from his own novel. Cast: Kirk Douglas, Milly Vitale, Paul Stewart, Joey Walsh, Alf Kjellin.

Act of Love. United Artists. Produced and directed by Anatole Litvak. Screenplay by Irwin Shaw from the novel *The Girl On*

The Via Flaminia by Alfred Hayes. Cast: Kirk Douglas, Dany Robin, Barbara Laage, Robert Strauss, Gabrielle Dorziat, Gregoire Aslan.

1954

Ulysses. A Lux Film distributed by Paramount. Produced by Dino De Laurentiis and Carlo Ponti in association with William Schorr. Directed by Mario Camerini. Screenplay by Franco Brusati, Mario Camerini, Ennio de Concini, Hugh Gray, Ben Hecht, Ivo Perilli and Irwin Shaw. Cast: Kirk Douglas, Silvana Mangano, Anthony Quinn, Rossana Podesta, Sylvie, Daniel Ivernel.

20,000 Leagues Under The Sea. A Walt Disney Production. Directed by Richard Fleischer. Screenplay by Earl Fenton from the book by Jules Verne. Cast: Kirk Douglas, James Mason, Paul Lukas, Peter Lorre, Robert J. Wilke, Carleton Young, Ted de Corsia.

1955

The Racers. 20th Century-Fox. Produced by Julian Blaustein. Directed by Henry Hathaway. Screenplay by Charles Kaffnab from the novel by Hans Ruesch. Cast: Kirk Douglas, Bella Darvi, Gilbert Roland, Cesar Romero, Lee J. Cobb, Katy Jurado.

Man Without A Star. Universal. Produced by Aaron Rosenberg. Directed by King Vidor. Screenplay by Borden Chase and D. D. Beauchamp from the novel by Dee Linford. Cast: Kirk Douglas, Jeanne Crain, Claire Trevor, William Campbell, Richard Boone.

The Indian Fighter. A Bryna Production, distributed by United Artists. Produced by William Schorr. Directed by Andre de Toth. Screenplay by Frank Davis and Ben Hecht. Cast: Kirk Douglas, Elsa Martinelli, Walter Abel, Walter Matthau, Diana Douglas.

1956

Lust For Life. MGM. Produced by John Houseman. Directed by Vincente Minnelli. Screenplay by Norman Corwin from the novel by Irving Stone. Cast: Kirk Douglas, Anthony Quinn, James Donald, Pamela Brown, Everett Sloan, Niall MacGinnis.

1957

Gunfight At The OK Corral. A Hal B. Wallis Production, distributed by Paramount. Directed by John Sturges. Screenplay by Leon Uris. Cast: Burt Lancaster, Kirk Douglas, Rhonda Fleming, Jo Van Fleet, John Ireland, Lyle Bettger, Frank Faylen, Earl Holliman.

Top Secret Affair. Warner Bros. Produced by Milton Sperling and Martin Rackin. Directed by H. C. Potter. Screenplay by Roland Kibbee and Allan Scott based on the novel *Melville Goodwin, USA* by John P. Marquand. Cast: Susan Hayward, Kirk Douglas, Paul Stewart, Jim Backus, John Cromwell, Roland Winters.

Paths of Glory. A Harris-Kubrick Production, distributed by United Artists. Produced by James B. Harris. Directed by Stanley Kubrick. Screenplay by Kubrick, Calder Willingham and Jim Thompson from the novel by Humphrey Cobb. Cast: Kirk Douglas, Ralph Meeker, Adolphe Menjou, George Macready, Wayne Morris, Richard Anderson, Joseph Turkel.

1958

The Vikings. A Bryna Production, distributed by United Artists. Produced by Jerry Bresler. Directed by Richard Fleischer. Screenplay by Calder Willingham from the novel *The Vikings* by Edison Marshall. Cast: Kirk Douglas, Tony Curtis, Ernest Borgnine, Janet Leigh, James Donald, Alexander Knox, Frank Thring.

1959

Last Train From Gun Hill. A Hal B. Wallis Production, distributed by Paramount. Directed by John Sturges. Screenplay by James Poe. Cast: Kirk Douglas, Anthony Quinn, Carolyn Jones, Earl Holliman, Brad Dexter.

The Devil's Disciple. A Hecht-Hill-Lancaster Films and Brynaprod co-production, distributed by United Artists. Produced by

Harold Hecht. Directed by Guy Hamilton. Screenplay by John Dighton and Roland Kibbee based on the play by George Bernard Shaw. Cast: Burt Lancaster, Kirk Douglas, Laurence Olivier, Janette Scott, Eva LeGallienne, Harry Andrews, Basil Sydney, George Rose.

1960

Strangers When We Meet. A Bryna-Quine Production, distributed by Columbia Pictures. Produced and directed by Richard Quine. Screenplay by Evan Hunter from his own novel. Cast: Kirk Douglas, Kim Novak, Ernie Kovaks, Barbara Rush, Walter Matthau, Virginia Bruce.

Spartacus. A Bryna Production for Universal-International. Executive Producer, Kirk Douglas. Produced by Edward Lewis. Directed by Stanley Kubrick. Screenplay by Dalton Trumbo from the novel by Howard Fast. Cast: Kirk Douglas, Laurence Olivier, Jean Simmons, Tony Curtis, Charles Laughton, Peter Ustinov, John Gavin, Nina Foch, Herbert Lom, John Ireland, John Dall, Charles McGraw.

1961

The Last Sunset. A Brynaprod, SA Production for Universal-International. Produced by Edward Lewis. Directed by Robert Aldrich. Screenplay by Dalton Trumbo from the novel *Sundown At Crazy Horse* by Howard Rigsby. Cast: Rock Hudson, Kirk Douglas, Dorothy Malone, Joseph Cotten, Carol Lynley, Neville Brand, Regis Toomey, Rad Fulton.

Town Without Pity. A Mirsch Production in association with Gloria Films (Munich), distributed by United Artists. Produced and directed by Gottfried Reinhardt. Screenplay by Silvia Reinhardt and George Hurdalek from the novel *The Verdict* by Manfred Gregor. Cast: Kirk Douglas, Christine Kaufmann, E. G. Marshall, Robert Blake, Richard Jaekel, Frank Sutton, Mal Sondook, Barbara Ruetting.

1962

Lonely Are The Brave. A Joel (Kirk Douglas) Production for Universal-International. Produced by Edward Lewis. Directed by David Miller. Screenplay by Dalton Trumbo from the novel *Brave Cowboy* by Edward Abbey. Cast: Kirk Douglas, Gena Rowlands, Walter Matthau, Michael Kane, Carroll O'Connor, William Schallert, Karl Swenson.

Two Weeks In Another Town. MGM. Produced by John Houseman. Directed by Vincente Minnelli. Screenplay by Charles Schnee from the novel by Irwin Shaw. Cast: Kirk Douglas, Edward G. Robinson, Cyd Charisse, George Hamilton, Dahlia Lavi, Claire Trevor, James Gregory, Rosanno Schiaffino.

1963

The Hook. A Pelberg-Seaton Production, from MGM. Produced by William Perlberg. Directed by George Seaton. Screenplay by Henry Denker from the novel by Vahe Katcha. Cast: Kirk Douglas, Robert Walker, Nick Adams, Enrique Magalona, Nehemiah Persoff, Mark Miller.

For Love Or Money. Universal. Produced by Robert Arthur. Directed by Michael Gordon. Screenplay by Larry Marks and Michael Morris. Cast: Kirk Douglas, Mitzi Gaynor, Gig Young, Thelma Ritter, Leslie Parris, Julie Newmar, William Bendix.

The List Of Adrian Messenger. A Joel (Kirk Douglas) Production from Universal. Produced by Edward Lewis. Directed by John Huston. Screenplay by Anthony Villier from the novel by Philip MacDonald. Cast: George C. Scott, Dana Wynter, Clive Brook, Herbert Marshall, John Huston and Kirk Douglas. Guest stars: Tony Curtis, Burt Lancaster, Robert Mitchum, Frank Sinatra.

1964

Seven Days In May. A Seven-Arts-Joel Production distributed by Paramount. Produced by Edward Lewis. Directed by John Frankenheimer. Screenplay by Rod Sterling from the novel by Fletcher Knebel and Charles W. Bailey. Cast: Burt Lancaster, Kirk Douglas, Frederic March, Ava Gardner, Edmond O'Brien, Martin Balsam, George Macready.

1965

In Harm's Way. A Sigma Production from Paramount. Produced and directed by Otto Preminger. Screenplay by Wendall

Mayes from the novel by James Bassett. Cast: John Wayne, Kirk Douglas, Patricia Neal, Tom Tryon, Paula Prentiss, Brandon De Wilde, Jill Hayworth, Dana Andrews, Stanley Holloway, Burgess Meredith, Franchot Tone.

The Heroes Of Telemark. A Benton Film Production, distributed by Columbia Pictures (in USA) and Rank (in UK). Produced by S. Benjamin Fisz. Directed by Anthony Mann. Screenplay by Ivan Moffat and Ben Barzman from the books *Skis Against The Atom* by Knut Haukelid and *But For These Men* by John Drummond. Cast: Kirk Douglas, Richard Harris, Ulla Jacobsson, Michael Redgrave, David Weston, Anton Diffring, Eric Porter, Mervyn Johns.

1966

Cast A Giant Shadow. A Mirisch-Llenroe-Batjac Production from United Artists. Produced, directed and written by Mel Shavelson from the book by Ted Berkman. Cast: Kirk Douglas, Senta Berger, Angie Dickinson, James Donald, Frank Sinatra, Yul Brynner and John Wayne.

Is Paris Burning? A Transcontinental Films-Marianne Production from Seven-Arts-Ray Stark, distributed by Paramount. Produced by Paul Graetz. Directed by Rene Clement. Screenplay by Gore Vidal and Francis Coppola, from the book by Larry Collins and Dominique Lapierre. Cast (in alphabetical order): Jean-Paul Belmondo, Charles Boyer, Leslie Caron, Jean-Pierre Cassel, George Chakiris, Alain Delon, Kirk Douglas, Glenn Ford, Gert Frobe, E. G. Marshall, Yves Montand, Anthony Perkins, Simone Signoret, Robert Stack, Marie Versini, Skip Ward, Orson Welles.

1967

The Way West. A Harold Hecht Production, from United Artists. Directed by Andrew V. McLaglen. Screenplay by Ben Ladlow and Mitch Linderman, from the novel by A. B. Guthrie. Cast: Kirk Douglas, Robert Mitchum, Richard Widmark, Lola Albright, Michael Witney, Sally Field, Katherine Justice, Stubby Kaye.

The War Wagon. A Batjac-Marvin Schwartz Production, distributed by Universal-International. Directed by Burt Kennedy. Screenplay by Clare Huffaker from the novel *Badman*. Cast: John Wayne, Kirk Douglas, Howard Keel, Keenan Wynn, Bruce Cabot, Valora Noland, Gene Evans, Joanna Barnes, Bruce Dern.

1968
A Lovely Way To Die. Universal. Produced by Richard Lewis. Directed by David Lowell Rich. Screenplay by A. J. Russell. Cast: Kirk Douglas, Sylvia Koscina, Eli Wallach, Kenneth Haigh, Martyn Green, Sharon Farrell.

1969
The Brotherhood. A Brotherhood Company Production for Paramount. Produced by Kirk Douglas. Directed by Martin Ritt. Screenplay by Lewis John Carlino. Cast: Kirk Douglas, Alex Cord, Irene Papas, Luther Adler, Susan Strasberg, Murray Hamilton, Eduardo Ciannelli.

The Arrangement. Warner Bros. Produced, directed and written by Elia Kazan from his own novel. Cast: Kirk Douglas, Faye Dunaway, Deborah Kerr, Richard Boone, Hume Cronyn, Michael Higgins.

1970
There Was A Crooked Man. Warner Bros-Seven Arts. Produced and directed by Joseph L. Mankiewicz. Screenplay by David Newman and Robert Benton. Cast: Kirk Douglas, Henry Fonda, Hume Cronyn, Warren Oates, Burgess Meredith, John Randolph, Arthur O'Connell.

1971
A Gunfight. A Harvest-Thoroughbred-Bryna Production from MGM. Produced by Ronnie Lubin and Harold Jack Bloom. Directed by Lamont Johnson. Screenplay by Harold Jack Bloom. Cast: Kirk Douglas, Johnny Cash, Jane Alexander, Raf Vallone, Karen Black.

The Light At The Edge Of The World. Bryna Production Inc., Jet Films, SA (Spain) and Triumfilm (Vaduz). Produced by Kirk

Douglas. Directed by Kevin Billington. Screenplay by Tom Rowe from the novel by Jules Verne. Cast: Kirk Douglas, Yul Brynner, Samantha Eggar, Jean Claude Drouot, Fernando Rey.

Catch Me A Spy. Ludgate Films (London), Capitole Films (Paris) and Bryna co-production. Produced by Steven Pallos and Pierre Braunberger. Directed by Dick Clement. Screenplay by Dick Clement and Ian La Frenais, from the novel by George Marton and Tibor Meray. Cast: Kirk Douglas, Marlene Jobert, Trevor Howard, Tom Courtney, Patrick Mower.

1972

A Man To Respect. Verona Productions-Orion Film Productions. Directed by Michele Lupo. Screenplay by Mino Roli, Nici Ducci and Michele Lupo. Cast: Kirk Douglas, Guiliano Gemma, Florinda Bolkan.

1973

Scalawag. Bryna/Inex-Oceania. Produced by Anne Douglas. Directed by Kirk Douglas. Screenplay by Albert Maltz and Sid Fleisherman. Cast: Kirk Douglas, Mark Lester, Neville Brand, Lesley-Anne Down.

Cat and Mouse (also known as *Mousey*). Made for television movie. Directed by Daniel Petrie. Cast: Kirk Douglas, Jean Seberg, John Vernon.

1975

Once Is Not Enough. Paramount/Sujac/Aries. Produced by Howard Koch. Directed by Guy Green. Screenplay by Julius J. Epstein from the novel by Jacqueline Susann. Cast: Kirk Douglas, Alexis Smith, David Janssen, George Hamilton, Melina Mercouri, Gary Conway, Brenda Vaccaro, Deborah Raffin.

Posse. Bryna/Paramount. Produced and directed by Kirk Douglas. Screenplay by William Roberts and Christopher Knopf. Cast: Kirk Douglas, Bruce Dern, Bo Hopkins, James Stacy, Luke Askew, David Canary.

1977

Victory At Entebbe. Warner Bros. Made for television on video tape and abridged and transferred to film for theatrical release. Produced by Robert Grunette. Directed by Marvin Chomsky. Teleplay by Ernest Kinoy. Cast: Elizabeth Taylor, Kirk Douglas, Linda Blair, Burt Lancaster, Helen Hayes, Richard Dreyfuss, Helmut Berger, Anthony Hopkins.

Holocaust 2000. Aston/Embassy. Produced by Edmondo Amati. Directed by Alberto DeMartino. Screenplay by Sergio Donati, Albert DeMartino, Michael Robson. Cast: Kirk Douglas, Simon Ward, Agostini Belli, Anthony Quayle, Virginia McKenna.

1978

The Fury. 20th Century-Fox. Produced by Ron Preissman. Directed by Brian De Palma. Screenplay by John Farris, from his own novel. Cast: Kirk Douglas, John Cassavetes, Carrie Sondgress, Charles Durning, Andrew Stevens, Amy Irving, Fiona Lewis.

1979

Cactus Jack (also known as *The Villain*). Columbia. Produced by Mort Engleberg. Directed by Hal Needham. Cast: Kirk Douglas, Ann-Margret, Arnold Schwarzenegger, Jack Elam, Paul Lynde, Strother Martin, Foster Brooks, Ruth Buzzi.

Saturn 3. ITC. Produced and directed by Stanley Donen. Screenplay by Martin Amis from a story by John Barry. Cast: Kirk Douglas, Farrah Fawcett, Harvey Keitel, Ed Bishop.

1980

The Final Countdown. United Artists. Produced by Peter Douglas. Directed by Don Taylor. Screenplay by David Ambrose, Gerry Davis, Thomas Hunter, Peter Powell. Cast: Kirk Douglas, Martin Sheen, Katharine Ross, James Farentino.

1981

Home Movies. Produced in collaboration with the Sarah Lawrence College. Directed by Brian De Palma. Cast: Nancy Allen,

Keith Gordon, Kirk Douglas, Gerrit Graham, Vincente Gardenia.

The Man From Snowy River. 20th Century-Fox. Produced by Geoff Burrowes. Directed by George Miller. Screenplay by John Dixon. Cast: Kirk Douglas, Jack Thompson, Tom Burlinson, Sigrid Thornton.

1983
Remembrance Of Love. Released on video by Videoform Pictures. Cast: Kirk Douglas, Pam Dawber, Robert Clary.

1985
The Shadow of God.

Draw! produced by Kirk Douglas for cable television. Starring Kirk Douglas and James Coburn.

1987
Tough Guys. Touchstone Pictures. Dirtected by Jeff Kanew. Cast: Kirk Douglas, Burt Lancaster, Charles Durning, Alexis Smith, Dana Carvey, Darlanne Fluegel, Eli Wallach, Monty Ash, Billy Barty.

Queenie. Miniseries made for television. Partial cast: Kirk Douglas, Mia Sara.

Index

206